D0182781

SARTRE'S
EXISTENTIALISM
AND HUMANISM

A BEGINNER'S GUIDE

SARTRE'S
EXISTENTIALISM AND HUMANISM

A BEGINNER'S GUIDE

GEORGE MYERSON

Hodder & Stoughton

A MEMBER OF THE HODDER HEADLINE GROUP

56364

Orders: please contact Bookpoint Ltd, 130 Milton Park, Abingdon, Oxon OX14 4SB. Telephone: (44) 01235 827720, Fax: (44) 01235 400454. Lines are open from 9.00–6.00, Monday to Saturday, with a 24-hour message answering service. Email address: orders@bookpoint.co.uk

British Library Cataloguing in Publication Data
A catalogue record for this title is available from The British Library.

ISBN 0 340 80418 1

First published 2002
Impression number   10 9 8 7 6 5 4 3 2 1
Year 2007 2006 2005 2004 2003 2002

Cover photo from Corbis Images.
Typeset by Transet Limited, Coventry, England.
Printed in Great Britain for Hodder & Stoughton Educational, a division of Hodder Headline Plc, 338 Euston Road, London NW1 3BH by Cox & Wyman, Reading, Berks.

CONTENTS

FOREWORD

Welcome to …

Hodder & Stoughton's Beginner's Guides to Great Works

… your window into the world of the big ideas!

This series brings home for you the classics of western and world thought. These are the guides to the books everyone wants to have read – the greatest moments in science and philosophy, theology and psychology, politics and history. Even in the age of the Internet, these are the books that keep their lasting appeal. As so much becomes ephemeral – the text message, the e-mail, the season's hit that is forgotten in a few weeks – we have a deeper need of something more lasting. These are the books that connect the ages, shining the light of the past on the changing present and expanding the horizons of the future.

However, the great works are not always the most immediately accessible. Though they speak to us directly, in flashes, they are also expressions of human experience and perceptions at its most complex. The purpose of these guides is to take you into the world of these books, so that they can speak directly to your experience.

WHAT COUNTS AS A GREAT WORK?

There is no fixed list of great works. Our aim is to offer as comprehensive and varied a selection as possible from among the books which include:

* **The key points of influence** on science, ethics, religious beliefs, political values, psychological understanding.

* The finest achievements of **the greatest authors**.

* The origins and climaxes in **the great movements** of thought and belief.

* The most provocative arguments, which have aroused **the strongest reactions**, including the most notorious as well as the most praised works.

* The high points of **intellectual style**, wit and persuasion.

READING THIS GUIDE

There are many ways to enjoy this book – whether you are thinking of reading the great work, have tried and want some support or have enjoyed it and want some help to clarify and express your reactions.

These guides will help you appreciate your chosen book if you are taking a course or if you are following your own pathway.

What this guide offers

Each guide aims:

* To tell the whole story of the book, from its origins to its influence.

* To follow the book's argument in a careful and lively way.

* To explain the key terms and concepts.

* To bring in accessible examples.

* To provide further reading and wider questions to explore.

How to approach this guide

These guides are designed to be a coherent read, keeping you turning the pages from start to finish – maybe even in a sitting or two!

At the same time, the guide is also a reference work that you can consult repeatedly as you read the great work or after finishing a passage. To make both reading and consulting easy, the guides have:

* Key quotations with page references to different editions.

* Explanations of key quotes.

Our everyday life is buzzing with messages that get shorter and more disposable every month. Through this guide, you can enter a more lasting dialogue of ideas.

George Myerson
Series Editor

A great work

* Sartre's *Existentialism and Humanism* has been probably the single most influential work by a modern philosopher, outside the walls of specialist philosophy. Written by a leading novelist as well as thinker, in the heightened moment after the Second World War, *Existentialism and Humanism* is a landmark work in modern ethics and also in modern literature.

* This intense work has defined for many the practical and theoretical meaning of 'existentialism', a major influence in the post-war period.

* But more profoundly, *Existentialism and Humanism* condenses Sartre's own personal project, as a philosopher, novelist, dramatist and activist.

Existentialism and Humanism gives a concrete – and often emotive – meaning to many of the big concepts of modern debates: responsibility and freedom, humanity and community. Only a great writer – as well as a major thinker – could have brought those ideas into such a sharp focus.

Key features

The aim of this guide is to bring home the dynamic challenge of Sartre's unfolding argument as a process of thought – and to place that process in its philosophical and political contexts. For this purpose a number of specific features are used.

Headings and Subheadings are used to enable you to follow the unfolding structure of the argument as a whole.

A small number of very brief key quotes are given, together with an accompanying 'Anatomy' explaining their particular significance.

The key ideas are summarized and placed in the wider context of Sartre's thought by the use of shaded boxes headed 'The Sartrean Project: Existential Principles ... Humanist Principles'. These boxes are also designed for ease of reference and application. In the central section, a particular key narrative is explained and here boxes convey the gist of 'the Sartrean parable'.

Brief key passages from Sartre's long philosophical treatise, *Being and Nothingness* and Martin Heidegger's *Being and Time* are also presented in quotation boxes for ease of reference.

NOTE ON ABBREVIATIONS
In the body of the guide, *Existentialism and Humanism* is abbreviated as *EH* and in references *Being and Nothingness* is given as *BN*.

A note on editions

This guide will particularly complement the excellent Methuen edition entitled *Existentialism and Humanism* (translation and introduction by Philip Mairet, 1948, 1973). There are a few brief quotes from that translation: the 'aims' set out at the top of each chapter include relevant page references showing the progression through the work as it corresponds to that text. The guide can equally be read with other versions such as that included in *Sartre: Six Essays in Existentialism* from Citadel Press (1993 – where the title is given as *The Humanism of Existentialism*).

Introduction: the moment of Sartre

AIMS

This short chapter tells the story of the original occasion on which Jean-Paul Sartre delivered his famous lecture entitled 'Existentialism and Humanism' in Paris in October 1945, immediately after the end of the Second World War, and sets it in context.

A key source is Anne Cohen-Solal's *Jean-Paul Sartre*, together with other biographical sources and Sartre's own writings.

THE OCCASION

Sartre's *Existentialism and Humanism* begins life as an announcement in the Paris press that on Monday 29 October 1945 at 20 hours 30 in the Central Hall at rue Jean-Goujon (metro Marbeuf) 'M. Jean-Paul Sartre parlera de "L'existentialisme est un humanisme" – Monsieur Sartre is going to speak on why his theory of existentialism is a form of humanism'. The occasion was being organized by the 'Club Maintenant', the 'Now Society'. The two organizers of the club, Jacques Calmy and Marc Beigbedder, were a bit nervous that they would not get a sufficient audience, which is why they took out advertisements in the big papers – *Le Monde*, *Le Figaro*, *La Liberation*, adverts that they could not really afford! They also left announcements in the bookshops of the Latin Quarter, Montparnasse and Saint-Germain-des-Pres.

Certainly, they hoped the title was striking. The wording had been agreed by Beigbedder and Sartre – after consideration of the blander 'existentialism'. This was already in the air as a word and Sartre was widely identified with it. But 'humanism' added a touch of spice – particularly since Sartre's novel, *Nausea*, featured a mocking portrayal of a character called the 'Autodidact' who is ridiculed for his 'humanism' – his sentimental optimism and naive trust in humanity.

The Club still had some nerves about covering its costs. They turned out to be right – but for the wrong reasons. What followed was a legendary event in the history of modern thought – a packed theatre, jostling, even blows exchanged, chairs smashed, women fainting in the crush. If they failed to recoup their costs it was not because nobody came: the ticket office was destroyed in the rush and so the tickets could not be sold. According to Sartre's biographer, Cohen-Solal, the organisers were by turns happy, worried and terrified by the uproar. Celebrity Paris was there – the publisher Gaston Gallimard and leading writers. The post-war intellectual era had begun.

The occasion is worth a pause. The evening followed a hot October day and the air was still heavy as a crowd gathered outside the hall, in their hundreds. The speaker, Sartre, came on his own – by metro from Saint-Germain-des-Pres. Looking down the street, seeing the huge crowd by the venue, he is said to have remarked that it must be a communist demonstration ready to denounce him – and to have considered going back home. Nobody recognized him – so he had to wait with the crowd, before letting himself be carried in the crush towards the hall. It took a quarter of an hour for him to get from the entrance to the platform where he was due to speak. More than an hour delayed, the room wildly hot, in an atmosphere of great intense excitement, the talk began.

The posture of the speaker has gone down in intellectual iconography – a symbol of a new era. Sartre spoke without notes and mainly with his hands in his pockets. He began by defending existentialism against the charges of others – and then launched into a detailed counter-argument. Packed together, the audience had to contend with analyses featuring many of the great names of modern thought, from Søren Kierkegaard to Martin Heidegger. In among these expected existential figures came references to Immanuel Kant and August Comte and a string of artists, thinkers and novelists, Voltaire and Diderot, Dostoevsky, Zola, Stendhal, Cocteau and

Picasso. Term by term, Sartre made his way across his own philosophical landscape: 'existence' and 'individual', 'responsibility' and 'anguish'. He told stories. He launched satires. He ended by sending out into the world the idea of a new 'existential humanism' and also trying to define the situation of a new being – the post-war European of 1945. There was not time for a proper discussion after as promised, though later the Club arranged a follow-up session.

Next morning Marc Beigbedder went to Sartre's favoured place, the Café des Flore, to apologize for the chaos and explain how difficult it had been to arrange things and also to add that they could not pay his honorarium – having nothing left after paying for the room, advertising and also all the breakages, including many chairs. Sartre replied 'Bah' never mind about the honorarium – 'c'est un succes!' and he pointed to a string of articles in the morning's press. Crowds had come 'to hear Jean-Paul Sartre' announced Maurice Nadeau in *Combat*, the journal edited by Albert Camus. All the articles talked with relish of the crowd, the panic – 'heat, fainting, ambulances'. The room was described as being like the setting for Sartre's play, *No Exit* – which takes place in a genteel hell, amidst heat, with no escape. One reporter compared the occasion to a scene from Groucho Marx's *Night at the Opera* and also to the climax of *Mutiny on the Bounty* – Sartre facing the crowd like Captain Bligh against the crew. Fifteen people were declared to have collapsed. Sartre was universally applauded for his 'courage' in facing the packed audience, the intense atmosphere and delivering a university course at the same time

It was the beginning of what Cohen-Solal calls the tidal wave of existentialism in that autumn – from that day Sartre was a celebrity and the lecture at 'Club Maintenant' became in retrospect the great occasion to have been at in 1945.

THE CONTEXT
The autumn of 1945 can be called the 'existential autumn'. The intellectual atmosphere belonged, of course, to a very particular

world. In that year, the Second World War ended. Germany had surrendered on 7 May 1945. Sartre's lecture took place in a France of rationed bread and power cuts, little more than a year after the liberation of the city from the Nazi occupation that lasted from 1940 to 1944.

The wider context can be gauged from Sartre's article of 24 August 1945 in the journal, *Clarté*, headed 'The Liberation of Paris' (reprinted in the Penguin collection, *Modern Times*). He wrote this piece on the first anniversary of the event, recording the celebrations and reflecting on their meaning. Turning back to the recent and yet also distant past, Sartre recalls how, as the Allied armies advanced on Paris, the Resistance rose against the Nazi occupiers in Paris. What was the point, he asked? Should they not have let the Allies save the city? For Sartre, the uprising had a deeper purpose: 'to reject destiny'. The result might have been a disaster: the Germans could have responded by reducing the city to rubble. But each man took the decision to act: 'Thus each one refused to place any hope except in himself.'

At heart, this is the image – the memory, the feeling – that animates Sartre's *Existentialism and Humanism* (*EH*), the idea of a chosen action, with no outside purpose to justify it in advance. The crowd who packed that lecture – and the many readers of the revised and printed text of 1947 – were entering into the world of that liberation, August 1944. Sartre was founding a new post war vision on a memory of the moment when the tide turned: 'The whole history of Paris was there, in that sun, on those loose paving stones.'

In the article, he affirms the 'profoundly human character' of the Resistance and their uprising – and it is to this human character that his humanism paid tribute.

That liberation was not really completed on those sunny days of August 1944 – it was still in progress in the autumn of 1945. Indeed, it was Sartre's inner message that the liberation process was always and everywhere in progress. Such a message had a particular resonance in the Europe – and the Paris – of that time. On 15 August 1945 Marshall Petain, head of state of the collaborationist Vichy regime, was condemned to death – a sentence commuted to life imprisonment by General Charles de Gaulle, the Free French leader who had become the new head of state. Others were not so fortunate: the Vichy leader, Pierre Laval, was executed on 15 October, a fortnight before Sartre's address. Meanwhile, the first post-war elections were held in October and long queues to vote were reported in the press. *EH* was first delivered at the cross-over moment where reconstruction meets liberation.

This was also the time when the full truth of the Second World War years began to emerge. The French press published its first revelations of the holocaust and the role of the collaborationist authorities in co-operating with it. In Albert Camus', journal, *Combat*, Jacques-Jean Bost sent reports from Dachau describing the gas chambers and the notice saying 'showers' outside. There was the lead-up to the Nuremberg trials of the German Nazi leaders, beginning just days after Sartre's talk, in November 1945. Throughout that autumn, moments of reconstruction are intertwined with the violent after-echoes of the liberation. On 22 November the novelist, Andre Malraux, became Minister of Information under de Gaulle in a government that included the communists lead by Maurice Thorez alongside de Gaulle's own conservative faction. Meanwhile, the editor, Robert Denoel, who had published fascist writings was murdered outside his home in Paris on 3 December. Malraux and Denoel: the public role of the writer could not be more graphically expressed than by these two figures from that autumn. Sartre was speaking in a moment when to be a writer, and a thinker, had an innate significance that has perhaps never been recaptured in the life of modern Europe.

Jean-Paul Sartre's own career itself came to an intense point of focus in that autumn. As we will see shortly, he was already an established novelist, dramatist and philosopher. But his most famous moment began in September 1945 with the publication of *The Age of Reason* and *The Reprieve*, two novels in what became the trilogy, *The Roads to Freedom*. These novels told the story of Mathieu Delarue, Sartre's fictional double – and the first two were vividly set in the time just before the war. The novels were followed in October by the first issue of *Modern Times*, a journal edited by Sartre and featuring, along with his own writings, the work of many of the leading French intellectuals including his partner Simone de Beauvoir, Camus and the leading philosopher, Maurice Merleau-Ponty. On 24 October 1945, Sartre gave a talk at a conference in Brussels – on 'existentialism', almost as big an occasion as the Paris gathering. Among that first audience was the leading English philosopher and novelist Iris Murdoch, a major source of Sartre's English influence in the immediate post-war period. According to Cohen-Solal, 'From September 1st to December 31st of 1945, not a single day went by which did not see in the press some reference to Sartre and to existentialism': this was indeed Sartre's existential autumn.

The press, newly liberated itself, conveyed a torrent of reviews of Sartre's new novels. But Sartre's work was also controversial. His fiction was denounced as 'smelling of shit' by one angry reviewer and in *Le Figaro* he was pilloried for crude style and a pessimistic outlook. *La Marseillaise* attributed to Sartre a malign influence on the young. For conservatives, he was the source of a false liberation, 'a theory which justifies every excess'.

This outpouring of reviews, often affirmative and sometimes abusive, ran from September 1945 into the autumn. It was here that Sartre became a public figure, almost a symbol of the unmuzzling of the French press after the occupation. The free press had been declared on 26 August 1944 and, with Malraux in the ministry in autumn 1945, there was a new freedom of expression. These were the days when language itself seemed set free: Raymond Millet in 1946 talked of 'the revolution that has transformed the French press'.

Sartre's talk fitted into this wider picture and was taken up in the tide of discussion. In the wake of the great lecture, there was a second occasion, 'Existentialism: For or Against' organized by Club Maintenant. This was the forum for the start of post-war French intellectual controversy. On one side, there were the defenders of Sartre and existentialism – including Colette Audry and Francis Jeanson. On the other side were the critics, including Emmaneul Mounnier and Julien Benda. This second occasion was also widely reported. There was a particularly famous review in *Samedi Soir* on 3 November 1945 in which Sartre's existentialism was denounced as not enriching the true French literature, as smuggling in ideas from Germany and Denmark. He was see as the importer of the German theories of Martin Heidegger and the Danish-Germanic thought of the nineteenth-century thinker Søren Kierkegaard. The conservative report asked angrily: 'What does this barbarous term "existentialism" mean?'

In this guide, we will be discussing Sartre's *Existentialism and Humanism* as a moment of crystallization – primarily within Sartre's own life and thought. It was also a point of crystallization in the wider life of French and western culture. In that same intense autumn, records Cohen-Solal, Jean Galtier-Boissiere wrote that for many existentialism had become a style of dress, a dance, a hairstyle, a district of Paris. The first intellectual fashion of post-war Europe had been born – but was it more than a fashion? How does the vision of that moment stand the test of time?

Jean-Paul Sartre – the road to *Existentialism and Humanism*

1

This chapter puts *Existentialism and Humanism* briefly into the context of Sartre's life and thought, before we move on to our guided reading.

* We look briefly at the biography of Sartre.

* The main subject of this chapter is 'The Sartrean project', the intellectual development to which the short text that is our subject bears witness.

* In addition, we identify Sartre's role in the history of existentialism.

JEAN-PAUL SARTRE: A BRIEF LIFE

Early years

* 1905   Jean-Paul-Charles-Aymand Sartre born in Paris on 21 July, son of Anne-Marie Schweitzer and Jean-Baptiste Sartre. Death of his father almost immediately.

* 1905–13   Brought up by his mother in the home of her father Charles Schweitzer, an Alsatian teacher. Known as little 'Poulou', the prodigy did not go to school in his earlier years.

* 1913   Enrolled in the Lycée Montaigne. But soon withdrawn from the school.

* 1915   Sent to school properly, Lycée Henri IV.

* 1917   Anne-Marie marries the conservative businessman Joseph Mancy. She is 34, he 43.

* 1920   Sartre returns to Lycée Henri IV as boarder.

Sartre's childhood is vividly evoked in his autobiography *Words*, written mainly in 1953, in the period after our text. In that account, Sartre says several things that are significant for *EH*. In particular, he reflects on the intertwining of his birth and the death of his father. He was born into 'Nights of vigil and worry' for his mother – and he remarks acerbically that 'I did my best to die too: from enteritis and perhaps from resentment.' Sartre is clear that he still thinks under the sign of his birth, a peculiar and empty freedom haunts his life:

> *I never stopped creating myself; I was both giver and gift. If my father had lived, I would have known my rights and duties.*

He tells of a childhood of books – reading above the city, above the world:

> *Every man has his natural place; it is not pride or worth that settles its height: childhood decides everything. Mine is a sixth floor in Paris with a view of the rooftops.*

The main theme of the autobiography, though, is Sartre's own hollowness – the way his life became a pretence, in the face of adult representations of him as a prodigy:

> *At first, I was sound as a bell: a little humbug who knew how to stop in time. But I stuck at it: I remained a good scholar even in bluff.*

Even the child is seen as responsible for his own genuineness – and his own inauthenticity. Here too, as we will see, Sartre's *EH* bears witness to his sense of his own life.

After the childhood, comes the time of the stalled yet promising young adulthood.

Towards recognition

✳ 1923   First published story, 'The Angel of Morbidity', *The Review Without Title*.

* 1924   Succeeds in exam to enter the elite École Normale Supérieure.

* 1924–8   Boarder and student at École.

* 1929   First meeting with his lifelong companion, lover and collaborator, Simone de Beauvoir, student at ENS.

* 1929   In November, begins 18 months' military service.

* 1931–3   Teacher at Le Havre Lycée.

* 1933–4   Stays in Berlin.

* 1934–6   Returns to Le Havre to teach. De Beauvoir in Rouen.

* 1936–7   Teacher in Laon, north-east of Paris. De Beauvoir in Paris.

* 1936   Publishes *Imagination* in August, a rewrite of an earlier essay on consciousness based on German philosophy, especially Husserl.

* 1937   Publishes story 'The Wall' in *Nouvelle Revue Française*.

* 1937   Teaching at Lycée Pasteur in Paris.

* 1938   *Nausea* published by Gallimard. Nominated for Goncourt Prize, praised by Camus, Blanchot and others.

This novel, *Nausea*, is the true beginning of the world's Sartre. It tells the story of Antoine Roquentin, an isolated man, living in Bouville – mudville – a version of Le Havre where Sartre had worked. We follow Roquentin's inner struggles with a desperate condition: 'Things are very bad: I've got it, that filthy thing, the Nausea'

At the climax of the novel, there is a famous scene in which Roquentin experiences the terrifying blankness of the world's existence:

The root of the chestnut tree plunged into the ground just underneath my bench. I no longer remembered that it was a root.

This vision, too, remains central to *EH*. The novel also features a sad character, called the Autodidact, who is made into the voice of a 'humanism' that Sartre – and Roquentin – mock. As we saw, this was one reason why Beigbedder was keen on the title that yoked together existentialism with humanism.

The war years were the time when Sartre's thinking formed.

The war

* 1940   *The Psychology of Imagination* expands and revises his treatment of human consciousness.

* 1940   23 May Death of Paul Nizan, a close friend, shot while acting as interpreter with the British.

* 1940   Paris falls on 14 June. On June 21 Petain signs Armistice with the Germans and France falls. Sartre is taken prisoner to Stalag 12D near Trier in Germany.

* 1940-1   Writes 'almost a million and a half words' according to Gerassi. Finishes *The Age of Reason*, drafts much of *Being and Nothingness*, writes and performs *Bariona*.

* 1941   In mid-March uses faked documents to leave camp and returns to Paris.

* From 1941 Forms 'Socialism and Liberty' resistance group with de Beauvoir, Merleau-Ponty and others.

* 1941   In autumn, teacher at Lycée Condorcet in Paris.

* 1943   *Being and Nothingness* published by Gallimard. Meets Albert Camus who is organizing the journal *Combat* and publishing works including *The Outsider* and *The Myth of Sisyphus*.

* 1943   Sartre's play *The Flies* opens in Paris, a pro-resistance work part of the changing climate as the Allies begin to turn the war.

* 1944   27 May First performance of *In Camera (No Exit)*. Finishing drafts of *The Age of Reason* and *Iron in the Soul*.

From Sartre's *War Diaries*, we get glimpses of the emergence of the vision to which his talk testifies. There is a struggle to rethink the concept of humanity itself, a struggle both philosophical and personal:

> *Tuesday November 21st 1939: The synthetic object is soon found: it is humanity. But this expression 'humanity' may have many meanings ...*

There is also a powerful feeling for immediate experience, the fact of existing in the world:

> *December 23rd 1939: An antiseptic, charming cold: the kind of cold of local anaesthetics, chilled meats, liquefied gases. One can feel its density when one walks on the road ...*

The writings – and the ideas – that burst upon the world in the autumn of 1945 were conceived and executed in the flurry of the war:

> *March 15th ... after lunch in overcoats, loaded down with satchels, gas mask and helmet ... two buses showed up into which we piled. The trip was as short as the wait was long. Yet I had time to plot out a prologue to* The Age of Reason ...

THE SARTREAN PROJECT: AN INTRODUCTION

From this period, there emerges a particular development – which we will call 'the Sartrean project' – of which *EH* is the great public expression, the symbol, the crystallization for the world. 'The Sartrean project' is something different from a 'normal' body of work. It is not an oeuvre or a sequence of books. In Sartre's own theory, the idea of the 'project' is very important (*Being and Nothingness* [*BN*] Part IV, especially pp.496–509). It is his way of talking about the process by which individuals give their own meaning to life, to their world. Conventionally, we think of giving meaning as a reflective activity. It is something you 'do' by thinking about your life or your experience, by interpreting memories or images. The Sartrean project is something else. It is not contemplation or interpretation, but making, shaping – it is a 'creative' process, to take another concept that will be central to our discussion of *EH*.

Sartre's writing from this phase has this character of being a personal project – fiction, dramas, essays, apparently abstract philosophical treatises, journalistic travel snippets – they come pouring out. Especially they come pouring out in the period of to which *EH*, our chosen text, belongs. This work testifies to a wider process, a fiercely energetic process of creative self-expression and self-definition in the world. You cannot really understand the peculiar impact of this little and in some way slight text outside the context of that wide process: the Sartrean project.

EH is not really a summary of a previously defined Sartrean philosophy – called, say, 'existentialism'. At points, Sartre does give the impression that this is what he is doing in *EH*. In fact, there is not really a predefined Sartrean philosophy to summarize – in the way that there would have been if the lecture had been given, say, by Sartre's German contemporary, Martin Heidegger, or if it had been a statement by another modern thinker, like Freud – at certain stages in his career – or even Camus. Despite appearances, Sartre does not really have a worked out and finished system to explain to his audience. If he had, then the effect would probably have been clearer, but it would also have been have less electric.

EH is a moment within a process, not a summary of a system but a peculiarly charged centre. In this guide, we will be using the image of 'crystallization' to describe the relation between *EH* and the wider Sartrean project to which it belongs and which it transfigures, briefly, into a world view. Each argument of *EH* is like a seed crystal dropped into the bubbling chemical process of Sartrean thought and feeling. Around these crystals, new reactions occur and magical crystals begin to form, points of diamond-shaped clarity. This text is not a summary, but a new crystallization – or a series of crystallizations. Around the seed crystals form delicate and sometimes fragile ideas and images. These are momentary effects, in some ways. The clarity does not last. The Sartrean project swept on and left these moments of lucid vision far behind.

The largest work in that project is *Being and Nothingness* and it is to that great opus that we will be consistently referring throughout our reading of *EH*. *Being and Nothingness*, written in the early years of the Second World War, looks like a monument of abstract philosophizing. Certainly the arguments employ a forbiddingly dense and technical terminology. Furthermore, there is implicit in *Being and Nothingness* a dialogue with an even more forbidding philosophical masterwork, Martin Heidegger's *Being and Time*, which Sartre had encountered in the 1930s and which dates from 1926. On the face of it, the connection seems strange: Sartre – the intellectual symbol of the French resistance, left, radical; Heidegger, a member of Nazi Party, rector of the University of Marburg under Hitler, at times an advocate of the fascist regime within German higher education. Heidegger – the betrayer of his own mentor, the Jewish thinker Edmond Husserl, a man never even really apologetic in the light of what emerged about Nazism. Yet Heidegger was the inspiration for the philosophical aspect of the Sartrean project in 1942, even while the German army had occupied his city of Paris. We will be looking at Sartre's relation to Heidegger in *EH* as we go through the text – and also at Heidegger's 'Letter on Humanism' written in critical response.

But first it is important to see how the Sartrean project emerges through *Being and Nothingness* – not in the normal philosophical mode, not as a series of carefully defended and defined propositions. Of course, the work is carefully argued in many places. But the whole text is also alive with feeling and with imagination and this is why *EH* has such a uniquely emotive and imaginative appeal, within its philosophical logic. In *Being and Nothingness*, Sartre tries to get hold of what he calls 'human reality' – a concept itself pointing back towards Heidegger. This 'human reality' is defined in terms of 'what it lacks' (p.89). Human reality – the world of human experience – is a reaching towards something that is not there, not yet present. Indeed the 'project' is one term for this reaching – this attempt to fill a gap, to complete what is not finished. Human reality starts as an encounter with a broken world, a world that is a fragment rather than a whole. Human reality tries to surpass this incomplete condition – in a process that reaches towards satisfaction, completeness or finality. If a person ever succeeded, she would become 'the particular being' which would at last 'be what it is'. If we overcame our situation, finally, we would have a feeling – a feeling that at last I had become myself, everything in my world was an expression of me and everything of me had at last come into expression in my world.

We do not arrive, according to Sartre. We will never get home, back to the world in which we are complete or forward to it. Instead, most of the time, people create 'constructions' to hide what Sartre calls the 'anguish' (*BN*, p.43) of their situation, being incomplete and demanding completeness. We are never going to arrive, because we *are* the incompleteness – that is how it is, to be human. Even our attempts to pretend that we are satisfied or stable will fail. We know that this anguish is there or that it will return.

Sartre's existentialism is defined by the pursuit of an impossible goal, being what one is. The philosophy of being is also centrally about non-being, nothingness. We never experience our own full being.

This ambivalent vision, the Sartrean project, was perfectly attuned to the atmosphere of the existential autumn of 1945, when Sartre came to give it fully public expression.

As we have remarked, the moment of *EH* is the pause just before reconstruction – it is a work for a world on the eve of reconstruction, poised between devastation and renewal. It is in that silence that *EH* speaks and from that moment that its vision catches fire. But the wider project was really formed in the heat of the war years.

Sartre answered a need. Europe itself was in need of a 'project' and Sartre's approach perfectly caught this need – and gave expression to it. Yet as we have already hinted, Sartre spoke in such dark terms that you might think there would be something disabling rather than inspiring in his arguments. Sartre certainly never flinches in the face of ideas or images that others might find repellent or even unbearable. What, for example, about love, romance? One of the most important aspects of the Sartrean project is that it engages with personal relations and not just political or philosophical theories and ideas. But the engagement is unremittingly grim. The world of interpersonal relations seems to consist of a kind of inevitable exploitation, at best a mutual exploitation: 'Desire is a consciousness which makes itself body in order to appropriate the Other's body' (*BN*, p.389).

But perhaps it was the resistance to romance that made Sartre inspiring: that was not a moment at which easy romanticism seemed plausible or relevant. It is also crucial that the project is interwoven of fiction and philosophy. Though the terms may often be dark, there is a kind of affirmation at work within them. It is from the novels, especially, that the Sartrean project gives birth to a distinctive form of modern heroism – the existential hero.

Here let us briefly consider *The Age of Reason*, whose publication formed the immediate prelude to *EH* in that autumn. At the start of the story, in the summer of 1938, Mathieu Delarue is 35, a philosophy teacher at the Lycée Buffon in Paris. He hasn't married, to the annoyance of his respectable lawyer brother, Jacques. He has a long-standing commitment to his lover Marcelle and at the same time he pursues the younger Ivich, a Russian student in Paris. As the novel begins, Marcelle tells Mathieu that she is pregnant. Stunned and also appalled, he presumes that the thing to do will be to arrange an abortion, currently illegal. This sets up the tortuous encounters in which Mathieu's commitment to his own freedom – and his notion of authenticity – are challenged and stretched to their limits.

For example, here we see him in a nightclub – with Ivich and her brother, Boris, and her lover, Lola. Ivich suddenly reaches out and sticks a knife into her own hand – in a gesture of defiance towards the onlooking respectable Parisians. Mathieu responds:

> *He jabbed the knife into his palm, and felt almost nothing. When he took his hand away, the knife remained embedded in his flesh, straight up, with its haft in the air.*

> *'You see', said Mathieu, with clenched teeth, 'anybody can do that.'*

Is this freedom? Or is it mere pretence, bravado, a common need to impress the girls? Such 'gestures' belongs to the ambiguous realm of the existential hero: half-absurd and half-courageous. Like Mathieu, we can never decide on the meaning of such actions – except that they *are* moments of action, seized from the slow inertia of everyday life. In Mathieu Delarue, Sartre gave to his project a centre as open-ended and indefinable as the more abstract arguments of *Being and Nothingness*.

In the account that follows, *EH* will be explained in terms of this wider 'Sartrean project', rather than directly in terms of a system called 'existentialism'. The term 'existentialism' is one of Sartre's ways of defining – and perhaps of publicizing – this difficult project. But the heart, both logical and emotional, is more distinctive, more personal. For example, Sartre makes his German contemporary,

Heidegger, into a key source for what he calls 'existentialism' – and it would be possible to tell a story of a philosophical movement unfolding from Heidegger to Sartre and beyond. But we will see how, in fact, Sartre consistently remakes ideas which begin with Heidegger. There is really no single 'philosophy' uniting these thinkers – rather a tense dialogue, often a contrast or a conflict across a shared language.

Take briefly a key moment from Heidegger's *Being and Time*. In the opening sections, he declares that his purpose is an 'Exposition of the question of the meaning of being'. He is going to expound for the reader 'The necessity, structure and priority of the question of being'. We have already seen that 'being' is indeed a central term for the Sartrean project, and one which came to him at least partly from Heidegger. But what a different feeling! Heidegger declares with authority that 'This question has today been forgotten' (p.21) and his task is 'working out the question of being' (p.36). Nothing could be further from the tense and intimate tone of Sartre's thought!

APPROACH OF THE GUIDE

In this guide, we will see:

* How *EH* belongs to Sartre's personal development and in particular how it has a unique role in 'the Sartrean project'.

* Within this perspective, we follow the *logic* of *EH*, a logic both intellectual and emotional. The aim of the arguments is to do justice to the facts – the experiences – of human suffering, without closing off the potential for affirmation.

Our commentary follows the structure of *EH*. We look first at how Sartre presents the charges against what he calls 'existentialism': that it removes the scope for affirmation by refusing to overlook the facts of suffering and the experiences of misery. Then we see how the unfolding counter-argument follows from the Sartrean project: that any attempt to achieve affirmation is bound to fail unless it starts from a recognition of the suffering, the reasons for not affirming.

After the charges, Sartre gives his account of 'existentialism', which, we will see, is really an extremely shorthand compression of the Sartrean project – in its downward swing, as a recognition of suffering. Then we focus on the central moment of *EH*: a story about Sartre as a giver of advice to a young man in trouble. This emerges in context as an example of not overlooking difficult facts or trying to give an easy solution. This story is the seed crystal at the centre of the whole crystalline formation.

Finally, we reach Sartrean *humanism* – as an affirmation capable of arising in the face of the recognized suffering. We look at his radical definition of what he calls *existential humanism*, as the re-expression of his own entire development.

Putting existentialism on trial 2

AIMS

* The guided reading begins with the early section of the text, in which Sartre announces his aim of defending 'existentialism'.

* We look at the personal basis for Sartre's account of the charges against this philosophy.

* Sartre's opening approach is placed in its wider philosophical context. (This chapter covers the arguments corresponding to Methuen edition, pp.23–5.)

I AM ACCUSED: SARTRE'S ORIENTATION

The occasion is a sell-out; the papers are full of reviews of the new novels. As Simone de Beauvoir says, the word 'existentialism' is on everyone's lips. Yet in his opening, Sartre presents himself to the audience – and then to his readers – as a man under siege: he has come, he says, to defend existentialism from widespread and often violent attack. He announces himself as the beleaguered spokesman for an embattled cause. This opening sets the tone for the whole argument and it is worth examining why Sartre sets up his talk in this negative way.

First, we can see a personal factor. Throughout his previous writings, one can detect a tendency to present important ideas and ideals in a defensive manner. One might even say that defensiveness under attack is the hallmark of a Sartrean intellectual personality. This is most vividly expressed by the story of Mathieu Delarue in *The Age of Reason*. As he seeks both the funds for Marcelle's abortion and the love of Ivich, Mathieu has a series of encounters in which he feels criticized, in which he has to defend himself and his beliefs. For example, when he is with Ivich: 'She's criticizing me,' thought Mathieu irritably.

In the famous opening scene, Marcelle too seems to accuse him:

> *'That is your ideal: you want to be nothing.'*

> *'To be nothing?' repeated Mathieu slowly. 'No, it isn't. Listen. I …*
> *I recognize no allegiance except to myself …'*

> *'Yes – you want to be free. Absolutely free. It's your vice.'*

> *'It's not a vice,' said Mathieu. 'It's … what else can a man do?'*

Mathieu is articulating key ideas of the Sartrean project, ideas of freedom and responsibility. But he is placed in the world as a man always under attack, always conscious of criticism, never expecting approval or agreement. Here he is with his brother, Jacques, the bourgeois:

> *'Come, shall I tell you the truth? I daresay you aren't lying to*
> *yourself at this precise moment: the trouble is that your whole life*
> *is built upon a lie.'*

> *'Carry on,' said Mathieu. 'I don't mind. Tell me what it is I'm*
> *trying to evade.'*

> *'You are trying,' said Jacques. 'to evade the fact that you're a*
> *bourgeois and ashamed of it.'*

Each time we see Mathieu, he is under attack from a different perspective. If it is not from the bourgeois angle of Jacques then it is from the communist position of his friend Brunet: if it is not from the cynical Ivich, then it is from the disillusioned Marcelle.

The opening strategy of *EH* is, therefore, an expression of a deep trait in Sartre's intellectual personality. But equally, the idea of 'defence' has ancient philosophical roots. In one of the most famous sources of western thought, Plato's *Apology for Socrates*, we see a philosopher formally defending himself, in a courtroom. Socrates has been accused of being a 'corrupter' of the youth of Athens. Sartre partly derives his strategy of defending existentialism and his own role as a teacher and writer, from this classic example. He will begin his talk by focusing not on himself, but on his accusers; this is precisely the strategy of Socrates:

What effect my accusers have had upon you, gentlemen, I do not know, but for my own part I was almost carried away by them; their arguments were so convincing.

(Plato's **Apology**)

Plato's Socrates creates a vivid sense of philosophy itself as an embattled calling:

Besides, there are a great many of these accusers, and they have been accusing me now for a great many years ...

As well as being deeply personal, Sartre's defensiveness recalls this ancient idea of the philosopher. The more authentic you are as a thinker, the more embattled you will be. The opening of Sartre's talk is the modern equivalent to the predicament of Socrates:

Very well, then; I must begin my defence, gentlemen, and I must try, in the short time that I have, to rid your minds of a false impression which is the work of many years.

It turns out, to anticipate, that the substance of the charges against Sartre and existentialism matches pretty exactly the charge list against Socrates, as summarized by the accused himself:

Socrates is guilty of corrupting the minds of the young, and of believing in supernatural things of his own invention instead of the gods recognised by the state.

We have already seen how in that autumn, Sartre had been identified as a new influence on the minds of the young in the post-war world. He is going to respond directly to that charge at the centre of *EH* and in doing so he makes himself the inheritor of Socrates:

Then it would seem that the whole population of Athens has a refining effect upon the young, except myself; and I alone corrupt them. Is that your meaning?

THE CHARGES

Next, there is an account of the positions against which Sartre felt he had to defend his project. Existentialism faces, he declares two main critics:

* *Communism*: the communists were about to enter the French government and they were at the height of their intellectual influence. Much of Sartre's post-war career was to be a dialogue with the Communist Party. In 1945, Stalin's USSR was still an ally of Western Europe and the USA in the defeat of fascism. Intellectually, the Communist Party was in many ways a conservative force, deeply suspicious of modern art and of anything that looked elitist or at odds with the official line of the march of the masses to freedom under the Party.

* *Christianity and specifically Catholicism*: the Catholic Church was still powerful in France and there was an intellectual revival of Christianity in some circles after the war. For example, the Anglo-American poet and critic T. S. Eliot articulated the widely shared feeling that without religious tradition, there can be no values.

Running within these ideologies, a third enemy or accuser might be added:

* *Everyday common sense and respectable opinion*: Sartre also feels under attack from a kind of lazy acceptance of the world, a proverbial cynicism favoured by the press.

These accusers correspond closely to those confronting Socrates, who, as we saw, was also accused of encouraging the young to become over-questioning of religion and of political authority.

Let's now consider the list of charges against existentialism as Sartre reviews them. All the accusations share the claim that existentialism is purely negative and, worse, that it rules out anything of an affirmative nature – affirmation being understood in diverse ways.

Defeatism

The communist charge is, he remarks, that Sartre and something of his called 'existentialism' encourage gloomy defeatism instead of constructive hope:

> Anti-existentialism: First Principle
> **To think too hard is to induce despair.**
> **OR**
> **Existentialists have a 'Hamlet' complex.**

This first charge is, really, that existentialists are not able to take action; that they stand and wait or watch while the communists do what is necessary; that their approach is not really neutral at all, but defeatist. There is a class war and those who are not with the workers must be against them. Hence existentialism is a bourgeois doctrine – the kind of ideology that serves to justify leaving the workers to be exploited and worse. An attitude that finds universal support for the lethargy of the privileged.

Sartre presents the charge as if it were levelled against a general philosophy. In fact, he has been consistently aware that such an accusation could be made to his own work. For example, in the *Age of Reason*, Mathieu is cornered by the communist Brunet who demands that he join the Party. He replies anxiously that 'I'm as angry as you', but that he does not have not 'enough reasons' to commit himself. Brunet's anger is given plenty of scope in the novel, and we are not left feeling comfortable about Mathieu.

Pathological ugliness

The second charge is presented as if it were made by Catholicism against existentialism in general. Here again the other side sees the existentialists as refusing to make any movement of affirmation. This time, though, the existentialists are seen as having a kind of fixation on the ugly sides of life. Just think how many appealing things there are in the world, say the hypothetical Catholic accusers – a kind of all things bright and beautiful, as Sartre makes it seem.

> Anti-existentialism: Second Principle
> *To neglect beauty is to show an obsession with ugliness.*

Existentialism is said to be all about the nasty side of life. For example, says Sartre, they are accused of ignoring the charm of babies. This, too, might be particularly an objection to Sartre's own project and indeed it was a criticism made in reviews of his novels that September. In *Nausea*, Roquentin in fact struggles to overcome a tide of disgust in the face of the details of reality:

> *Smiles. His teeth are rotten … This fellow with the moustache has huge nostrils which could pump air for a whole family and which eat up half his face, but in spite of that he breathes through his mouth, panting slightly.*

The *Age of Reason* has many moments where characters are beset by a similar revulsion. One figure, Daniel, is the particular medium for this feeling of overwhelming ugliness:

> *Naked to the waist, Daniel was shaving in front of his wardrobe mirror. …in the faint rasp of the razor … The backs of his eyes were smarting from want of sleep, and he had a pimple under his lip, a tiny red spot tipped with white …*

Sartre's fiction wraps us – and him – in a cloud of intense and often repellent images.

Introspection

A third charge is attributed to both communists and Catholics. They are said to claim that existential philosophy is too introspective, too inward-looking. Existentialists are seen as ignoring the reality of the outside world and staying buried in the dreams of the inner world.

> ### Anti-existentialism: Third Principle
> **Introspection is a vice, not a source of insight.**

Existentialists are seen as frivolous, therefore, because they turn aside from what really matters, the real things of life. The existential world is too insubstantial. This philosophy over-dramatizes the anxious sense of being at a distance from reality that affects everyone at times.

Here, perhaps most deeply, it is really the Sartrean project that is in question. In *Being and Nothingness*, Sartre recalls the formulation of the French Renaissance philosopher, the rationalist Descartes: 'cogito ergo sum', 'I think, therefore I am'. Sartre talks of the human consciousness sometimes using Descartes' term, as the 'cogito', the 'I think'. In *EH*, existentialists are accused of being obsessed by this 'I think', this cogito – at the cost of social or spiritual awareness. In *Being and Nothingness*, Sartre is unrelenting in his emphasis on introspection, as both a method and a subject for his thought: 'I think, therefore I am. What am I?' (*BN*, p.80). Is this not an approach calculated to paralyze the world at the moment when hope and commitment are most needed?

This opening – with its stance of embattled defence and its list of charges – gives to *EH* the atmosphere of the climax to a courtroom drama. Ostensibly, it is existentialism that is on trial – an as yet undefined position in the argument. In practice, it is Sartre's own personal project – and also the whole tradition of western philosophy going back to Socrates.

3 How to be an existentialist

AIMS

* This chapter presents Sartre's fundamental statement of what is ostensibly 'existentialism' in general, on which he bases his defence.

* Four concepts are central to his account – and we will see how each concept acts, in fact, as a point of crystallization for the Sartrean project.

* The chapter focuses on each concept in turn, in a separate section, outlining Sartre's own definition, explaining its relation first to his own thought, then to other thinkers.

(This chapter covers the arguments corresponding to Methuen edition, pp.26–34.)

EXISTENTIALISM: A BLIGHTED CONCEPT?

Sartre moves on from the charge list. The term 'existentialist' has now become fashionable, he says, which is why there is such hostility. But what does this word really mean? In the fashion, yes, it seems to mean just taking the worst possible view of everything, being a misery or being cynical. An existentialist is someone who is always, on principle, expecting the worst.

Before giving his counter-definition, Sartre makes a basic division between religious and atheist existentialists. He sees the religious faction, identified with his contemporary Gabriel Marcel and with the German thinker Karl Jaspers, as an incomplete and inconsistent form of the theory. On the atheist and, in Sartre's view, consistent side, he includes above all Martin Heidegger, together with himself. The account which follows is explicitly from this atheistic side – recall, perhaps, that Socrates was accused of encouraging the young to disbelieve in the official gods!

Sartre then launches his counter-definition of this 'existentialism'. The argument is fluid, but at its heart are four key concepts.

EXISTENCE

Existence: the existential argument

Existentialism is an approach to existence:

KEY QUOTE

existence comes before essence.

(Methuen edn, p.26)

This is the most influential formulation in *EH*, the one that made it seem to articulate a coherent modern philosophy. Yet in many ways, the idiom is that of medieval theology. How can this be? How has a language that would have been recognizable to St Thomas Aquinas in the Middle Ages become the basis for an outlook that seemed definitively modern?

The terms are technical and they do originate in systematic theology. They also point back still further, towards the first great western philosophy, Plato's theory of forms.

Sartre gives an example: he tells the story of a paper knife, but it could on the face of it be any manufactured object. Take any article, the argument runs, that has been man-made. It came into the world in order to realize a conception that preceded it. This is true of very simple objects – like paper clips or razors – and of much more complex objects – like, we might add, the Internet or London University. Someone had an idea. Let's make something to keep these pages together. Let's set up an institution to teach physics. In all such cases, the conception comes before the entity. The paper clip comes into being as a reflection of an original idea. If it fails to express that idea, it is a failed paper clip. Unless it performs that function, the one designated for it, it has not carried out the destiny for which it was born.

The paper clip, in Sartrean terms, has an essence that comes before its existence. We know what it is supposed to be, before we make it. Therefore, we can judge any given paper clip by these prior standards. The same is true, albeit in a more complex way, of any human creation that embodies a human idea. But what about humanity itself? If there was a creator, who had an idea, then we are just like the paper clip. If God made us in the light of His idea, then He moulded our existence to fit an essence that came before it. Then our essence must have preceded our existence. There might be more abstract versions of this logic, even if we don't bring in so literally the notion of a creator. There might be an ideal 'form' of humanity – a human nature – of which each individual is merely an expression. This is a remote descendant of Platonic theory. Or there are more scientific-looking versions. There might be a human nature that finds expression in each of our lives. Many modern thinkers have adopted such an idea of human nature, even if they have not referred directly to God – Marx, for example, according to Sartre, had such a view of the human as a fixed nature.

For Sartre, existentialism is the reverse view: there is no concept of the human until we make one. Existentialists take their stand against all the 'that's human nature' arguments, whether directly religious or apparently secular. It all seems surprisingly technical, for a philosophy that has had such an emotional impact. But within the apparently technical terminology, this theory is fundamentally about a kind of suffering – it looks technical, but has a psychological and emotional point. This is the underlying reason why Sartre builds his Sartrean project on existential concepts.

Why is this a vision of suffering? Because it would be so much more comfortable if we could explain ourselves as the product of some previous decision, some external idea, some outside force. Take, for a further example, the role of 'race' in modern politics and culture. Often the notion of 'race' is used to 'explain' people or 'cultures'. I am like this because of my British nature or my Jewishness or my blackness. These explanations are used from different sides of the political spectrum, in different ways. There are both racist and anti-racist versions of the argument using race as a prior category. From Sartre's existential perspective, these arguments would ring hollow. Race is an attempt to smuggle back into the modern world a prior essence that determines the existence of individual people from outside and in advance of their choices. There is also a version of 'culture' that plays the same role in contemporary arguments. Why do I behave like this? Because of the culture to which I belong. In so far as culture seems to pre-determine my life from outside, then it is suspect from the Sartrean perspective.

There are, in fact, lots of concepts that play this role: race, culture, human nature, rights, God. Each of these concepts is a would-be 'essence', an idea which seeks to come before the existence of individual people. Such essences are wonderfully resilient. No sooner has one gone out of fashion, than we have come up with another. If the soul goes out of favour, then race comes into play. If race goes out of favour, then culture comes into play.

From Sartre's point of view, all of this shows that we are reluctant to see the existential predicament. Almost all the big political and cultural doctrines are attempts to evade that predicament: that our existence is prior to our essence, that we have not been made this way, but have made ourselves. Analyse any political or moral orthodoxy and it will betray this origin – in the evasion of the existential facts. Take for example a popular newspaper or the role of soap opera or reality television. Open the pages of the newspaper. This is how we are: men behave that way, women this way. Follow the soap story: why do the characters act like that? Because it's human nature. Their individual characters are like little packets of human nature. He is greedy, she is jealous. These are fixed natures and they reflect a general human essence.

Existence: the Sartrean project

There is a lot behind this brief argument about existence and essence. The key is that in the Sartrean project the priority of existence over essence is an emotionally charged idea, not a technical matter. This is really one way of putting a principle that Sartre tried out in several alternative versions.

Sartrean project: First Existential Principle
Existence gives me nothing in advance.

In the extended argument from which *EH* crystallizes out (*BN*, p.95ff) Sartre makes a division between 'being-in-itself' and 'being-for-itself'. The in-itself is the category of pure objects – these are gifted with what Sartre calls 'fullness'. They are entirely themselves and nothing else. That table is simply all table. Every particle of it is table and nothing is missing or awaited. Neither is there any mixture of anything else. By contrast, the 'for-itself' is Sartre's term for consciousness – we always experience our own being reflected back to our consciousness. We are not only here, we are aware of being here. That means that there is a gap in our being – we miss out on 'full equivalence'. Something is never quite there, for human beings. I am over here and the experience of which I am aware is at a slight remove. If only I could be right in the middle of that experience, instead of just to one side, being conscious of it! This is the 'being of consciousness' – a gap, a break, a division in being.

The in-itself is filled with its own essence: every particle of that tree is pure tree and the whole thing is entirely there. But I am different, standing here looking at the tree. I do not have the same kind of being. I am conscious of myself looking at it – so that the looking cannot be the whole of me, there must be a reserve, something apart. And then I am conscious of being conscious … there is no end to the recession. This is a kind of suffering, as well as a source of possibilities.

In the clipped arguments of *EH*, Sartre still conveys the urgency that belongs to the longer loop of his full reflections. This is not an answer or the basis of a system. My life remains a problem. For the tree, whose essence is given in its existence, there is 'not the tiniest crack through which nothingness might slip in'. It is this extraordinary poetry that lies behind the impact of *EH* – not the summary of a system, but a signpost to poetry and vision.

To exist without prior essence: this is both a blessing and a curse – it means that we alone are gifted with the capacity to lack part of ourselves. We do not yet have that full being which one day, we hope, we will experience. In that moment of fullness, I will be exactly and completely myself and that self will be entirely and completely human. As it is, I have to cast my thoughts and intentions forwards towards that fullness.

Existence: Sartre and Heidegger

This Sartrean project is always in dialogue with Heidegger – or includes a certain way of seeing Heidegger – not one, it turns out, that Heidegger accepted himself (later). The ideas we have been examining can also be seen as Sartrean creative appropriations of Heidegger. It is the strength of Sartre's philosophical personality that imposes itself in these encounters. And it is through that strength of personality that the Sartrean project imprints itself on 'existentialism'.

If one now turns to Heidegger, it is true – as Heidegger was to claim – that you can find a 'source' for Sartre's argument about existence and essence:

The essence of Dasein lies in its existence.

(Heidegger, *Being and Time*, p.67)

Dasein, 'being-there', is Heidegger's term for human reality: being-there is the human principle. The same terms are taken over by Sartre, yes. And the underlying point is related. Being human means coming into the world without the support of a prior definition or conception. Heidegger though has a different emphasis – he is not really talking in terms of absences, nothingness, cracks in being, deficiencies and hopes. Heidegger's world is more self-contained, more in balance, less tortured.

If you ask whether Sartre is 'getting Heidegger right', then you would have to say no, not really. Heidegger does not, in context, mean that there is a split in human reality – that we have to struggle towards fullness and can never arrive. He means that it *is* our being, to exist – and nothing more. This is us – Dasein, being-there. In tone, Sartre comes close to reversing Heidegger.

Here is Heidegger's version of the difference between being human and being an object – a table, a tree. Human beings have 'characteristics'. But these are different from what Heidegger calls the 'properties' of things. The characteristics of a human entity are – says Heidegger – 'in each case possible ways for it to be'. It could always be otherwise. So if you describe an entity as human, if you credit it with 'Dasein', then you are not defining its 'what' but outlining its 'Being'.

You can see how Sartre has woven his famous declaration in *EH* from the same material. But through the project, especially as formulated in full in *Being and Nothingness*, Sartre has given the ideas his own colouring, his own twist and weave. It's not really a question of getting Heidegger right or wrong – but of taking over a language and using it in his own voice, to say what he wants, rather than what Heidegger originally intended the same terms to say.

RESPONSIBILITY

Responsibility: the existential argument

Only one person can answer your questions for you: yourself. This is not only about general views and outlooks. Sartre has a very extreme conception of responsibility and again it is fundamentally dark. There is nothing in my life for which I am not responsible.

In Sartrean responsibility, I do not only choose specific actions. I have made myself this way; at some very fundamental level, I have chosen to be this kind of person. Of course there are circumstances and influences, but they never become excuses. Not only that – but I am responsible without limits. I can't make mistakes just for myself – they happen in the world and so they affect all the others. In fact, I can't see my own situation as personal at all.

This argument has deep roots in the early nineteenth-century philosopher Immanuel Kant:

> *I only ask myself whether I can also will that my maxim should become a universal law.*
>
> (Kant, *Grounding for the Metaphysic of Morals*, p.15)

By contrast, just consider the role that 'responsibility' plays in current political discourse. What it means to be irresponsible now is mainly a spectrum of violence from hooliganism to terrorism or a lifestyle that involves refusing to do a decent day's work. In this view, being responsible really means just living a conventional life. Nothing could be less like Sartrean responsibility.

Responsibility: the Sartrean project

In *EH*, Sartre is not so much arguing for a doctrine of responsibility as evoking the feeling of being responsible. Through the Sartrean project, there has run this *feeling* – it is at the heart of the distinctive emotional ambivalence of the Sartrean project. On the one hand, I am absolutely tied to my life, in every aspect – the whole of my being expresses my own decision and the same is true of each act or even feeling. Yet this is not simply a trap – on the contrary, this is my freedom. To the extent that I am not responsible, I cannot have been free either. If my act is the product of a situation or my character the outcome of circumstances, then my life is not truly my own doing or making.

Sartrean Project: Second Existential Principle

I am entirely responsible – this is my privilege and my burden as a human being.

These intense pages of *EH* are evoking an ambivalence that Sartre has been attempting to capture in many of the most intensely poetic moments of his work.

For instance, *Being and Nothingness* has an extraordinary image of a 'billiard ball' rolling over an almost smooth green cloth on a billiard table. Then there is a little wrinkle on that almost perfect surface. The ball swerves slightly to one side (*BN*, p.81). Sartre closes in on this tiny movement. Where has it come from? Whose future was it before it happened? You cannot say this little swerve was ever a 'possibility' belonging to the billiard ball – it never had within it the potential to swerve off course, it only had the property of rolling forward until the force exerted on it wore off. But you also could not say the wrinkle in the cloth had that 'possibility' in it either. It was just a hump of imperfection in the smooth greenness. It never had the potential to cause any change in the path of the ball. But then bring in a human observer – a 'witness'. From the observer's perspective, that possibility suddenly springs into existence. She sees the ball rolling, she remarks the fold in the cloth and from her point of view, there comes into being a 'possibility' – of the little swerve. It is a possibility that appears 'synthentically' – she creates it by weaving together all the elements of the event in a moment of perception.

It is worth unpacking these arguments by extending the example. Consider the same person in her own life. She is standing in a crowded room. There on the other side a face catches her attention. She pauses. In that moment, there is a 'possibility' of her going over and saying hallo – and another of her going and getting another drink instead. These possibilities belong to her being – even if there is no outside observer to witness the situation. This is the human condition, as expressed by the concept of responsibility that Sartre had developed:

> *the possibility ... belongs to certain beings as* their *possibility; it is the possibility which they are, which they have to be.*
>
> (*BN*, p.81)

She possesses her own possibilities – they are her responsibility.

> *In this case being sustains its own possibilities in being; it is their foundation ...*

This is Sartre's poetic-philosophical evocation of human responsibility: we sustain our own possibilities in being. They come into existence from our perspective, in our consciousness of our own life. Sartrean responsibility means just that: sustaining your own possibilities. There is no other sense in which that possibility of crossing the room exists, except within her experience. But within that experience it exists absolutely – it is as real as the tables and chairs and the shoe of the woman in front on which her eye also lingers.

At the heart of the Sartrean project is this ambivalent recognition of total responsibility – of sustaining our own possibilities in being.

There is a religious implication to this theme of responsibility. There can be no God who takes unto Himself this absolute responsibility. Those possibilities flow into being entirely through my consciousness – I make them necessary:

> *In a word, God, if he exists, is contingent.*

This is the basis of the atheism with which, in *EH*, Sartre has identified himself and his work.

Responsibility: Sartre and Heidegger

When we compare these Sartrean arguments with Heidegger on responsibility – we can see a Sartrean aspect to Heidegger and also a contrast. Heidegger was certainly a source for these ideas, as in this famous declaration about Dasein, being-there or human reality:

> *Furthermore, in each case Dasein is mine to be in one way or another. Dasein has always made some sort of decision as to the way in which it is in each case mine ...*
>
> (Heidegger, *Being and Time*, p.68)

Heidegger also has a vision of total responsibility – life is 'in each case mine'. But his approach has far less sense of isolation and even desperation that colours the Sartrean vision of responsibility. Heidegger seems to be talking about a natural situation, rather than a terrible predicament. No wonder he was reluctant to be bracketed under Sartre's existential banner!

ANGUISH

Anguish: the existential argument

Sartrean 'anguish' is not a passing emotion, neither are some people more inclined to it than others. For Sartre in *EH*, humanity is in anguish. This is his term for the universal experience. He does not mean merely that everyone has a tendency to feel miserable or that no one ever gets what he wants. He does not even mean, not directly, that we are all going to die, though anguish is connected with mortality. Anguish is the other side of our absolute responsibility. I make a decision and immediately I am responsible in total for its meaning in the world, its meaning for everyone else as well as for myself.

Let us elaborate with an example. I am walking down the street. A woman in colourful but ragged clothes holds out her hand for money. I think 'asylum seekers' – in the phrase of the day. Say I choose not to give her the money. For Sartre, I have just exercised my freedom on behalf of the entire future of the human race. In my moment of choice, I have committed humanity in general to a future where that is the way to act. The same incidentally is true the other way round – if I give the money. In my choice, the whole future lies coiled. In each decision, I commit the world to its future.

If you reply: come off it, no one else has made the choice. It's purely personal. Sartre replies: there are no purely personal decisions, in that sense, that they apply only to you. Each moment of decision is personal, in that an individual is responsible. But not in the other sense, that no one else is involved. On the contrary: everyone else is implicated, whether they like it or not and whether I like it or not.

Each choice has a limitless future. In every decision I am engaging in the making of the horizon for all of humanity. But there is still no way to justify my choices, finally. All I can do is stand by them, I will never be able to find any outside justification to lift from my shoulders the weight of the decision. I can point say – in the case of the 'asylum seeker' – to the words of government ministers – say, the Home Secretary has advised me not to give money to such characters. It is not good for them and it only encourages more incidents. I try to offload my responsibility I am only following advice, doing what I have been asked. But still I have to choose to follow the advice, in this particular situation, faced by this specific hand. Or the other way: Christianity says love thy neighbour. So I am going to give ... but again, I am making the choice to see Christianity in that way at this moment and to consider that the rule which counts for me.

Sartre gives more dramatic examples too. The leader who sends his followers into battle. Maybe all the manuals support his decision. Perhaps all the men are willing. Perhaps his whole nation is behind the war. Still, the choice remains his alone. Nothing can lift the burden from his shoulders. Neither for that matter does his responsibility lift an equal burden off each man individually. They have to decide whether to follow his orders, each one. Even if they will be shot instantly for desertion, they are still in the position of having to choose. Still, the leader has to stand by his moment – he cannot point to the freedom of others as an excuse.

Anguish: the Sartrean project

In Sartrean anguish, a series of futures unfolds – futures where this man is dead, instead of returning home; futures where the war is won instead of lost. But also more abstract futures – where the rule for human beings is to send others into battle, when the independence of the state is at stake, say, or when the man in charge decides or when the elected government has declared war in the proper manner.

Yet none of these futures is necessary. If I chose differently, then these futures would never come into being, on the horizon. Anguish is this relation to the future, in the countless moments of decision.

Sartrean Project: Third Existential Principle
Anguish is the experience of my freedom.

Anguish is the centre of Sartrean *psychology* – the psychology of freedom. It is the reason why happiness is not really a plausible aim for human beings – not a sufficient aim on its own. To the extent that you made happiness your entire goal, you would be doomed to failure. Because as a free being there would always be the anguish of making the limitless future in each instant's decisions. We cannot be perfectly happy without concealing from ourselves the weight of our freedom.

There are many evocations of this distinctive anguish in Sartre's fiction. In *The Reprieve*, Mathieu is sitting at a café table. This is the time of 'Munich' – the moment in the summer of 1938 when the British and French leaders attempted one final negotiation with Hitler. At this point in the novel, the talks seem to have failed. Hitler has announced the coming war. In fact, there will be a 'reprieve' – though that in turn gives way to the war. This is a complex game of futures – each emerging and fading in turn. The novel is all about futures that do not happen – what kind of reality they do and do not possess. Mathieu is thinking about his future, as he sits at that table. 'His future: peace, the future of the world, and Mathieu's future.' He suddenly feels that he has leaped ahead of his own future. Below him, he sees lying still, a 'crystalline' and peaceful future. That is the one with which he lived his life – and not just Mathieu, but the western world. Now he leaps ahead of that 'future' into a different prospect – the vista of the war. This is the moment when he realizes the self-deception of his previous life.

That crystalline peaceful world was not really a future at all. It was really just a frozen present tense – the endless continuation of the present moment. That is how the western world has lived its interregnum, between the wars – as if there were no real future, but only a continuous present. That still vista is not an experience of futurity at all. We cannot be truly calm and at ease in the face of a true recognition of futurity. The future is always different, it is always elsewhere. This sense of the future begins with this recognition that the present has limits – which we will not be living here for long.

Now Mathieu sees the approaching war not as a misfortune, but as 'the result' of his own life and all their lives. This dark world coming towards us is not someone else's world. It is our world. It is the world as we have made it, as we have chosen to live it. This future is our choice, though it is also entirely alien, apparently beyond our control. Here is the pure moment of anguish.

Ironically, by denying anguish – by refusing to see themselves as responsible for the future in which they will live – the inhabitants of the western world have created the terrible prospect that is about to make itself into their reality. There is an appalling price to pay for the flight from anguish.

Anguish: Sartre and Heidegger

Anguish is a Sartrean take on the idea more familiar in the German word 'Angst'. Heidegger has many vivid passages on this fundamental anxiety:

> *The turning away of falling is grounded rather in anxiety, which in turn is what makes fear possible. ... That in the face of which one has anxiety is Being-in-the-world as such.*
>
> (Heidegger, *Being and Time*, p.230)

But for Heidegger, anxiety – what Sartre calls anguish – is always a potential source of illumination:

> *Being-anxious discloses, primordially and directly, the world as world.*
>
> (Heidegger, *Being and Time*, p.232)

There is a contrast between the contorted paralysis of Sartrean anguish and the Heidegger's more bearable conception. Here too we can see how, under the heading of a shared 'existentialism', Sartre is really expressing a deeply personal project. He does take over some conceptions, particularly from Heidegger, but the tone, the feeling, the intensity, is his own.

ABANDONMENT

Abandonment: the existential argument

'Abandonment' is Sartre's way of describing an absence at the heart of our lives. Something is missing. I turn towards it and there is no response. For example, we might say, I am queuing in a busy shop. Everyone is looking tired and tetchy. People are beginning to complain. They shout at their children. They glare at the person unloading the trolley up ahead. But no one charges past, pushing everyone else over and hurtles out of the exit. No one pushes the others away or throws their tins through the window. There are countless moments like that in the fabric of what I experience as normal life. Here we are again, getting into our cars to go home in the evening. We sit angrily in our lines. We may hoot and perhaps shout. But we don't suddenly accelerate en masse and take our chances ... Each moment has countless possibilities that are not taken in it. It seems to me that something absolute must underwrite the awesome continuity of the real world. There must be some reason why so many people – in every hour of every 'normal' day – stick to the expected patterns.

In fact, Sartre says, there is nothing behind us. We just live that way. There are lots of little reasons – if I speed off with my groceries, I will be arrested and so on. But there is no one big reason. Nothing compels us all to be like this – to keep the rules or not. We are abandoned to our own freedom. Modern politics can be seen as a terrified flight from this abandonment – that we really are choosing at each moment to live like this, that there is no big reason, that we could in each instant choose to start over and live differently.

The main name, according to Sartre, for the missing big reason is: God. We have been abandoned by God.

KEY QUOTE

God does not exist, and ... it is necessary to draw the consequences of his absence right to the end.

(Methuen edn, p.32–3)

This is not only a theological observation. It is an everyday experience. We look around at our way of life. It seems so solid, so real. There are so many possibilities that never occur to us or only to those few others whom we count as mad or wicked or otherwise deviant. We feel that this way of life must be embedded in some giant ultimate explanation. We can't simply have decided to live like this. There must be a larger case. We must have followed instructions at some original point, to get to here.

According to Sartre's argument, the modern ruling class have hoped to get away with the disappearance of this God. It has become, he says, fairly conventional now to accept – openly or covertly – that there is no such presence in our lives. But, so what, say the modern bourgeois authorities! Maybe, it makes no difference. After all, we still have the old values and they are just as strong as ever. Sartre insists that without God, the old ethics is also doomed. There is nowhere for those old values to survive. If God is not in his heaven, then 'His' values have no home either. From this Sartrean perspective, most modern politics are an attempt to evade our state of ethical abandonment, to insist that the old values retain as much absolute force as they did in the past, when they issued forth from the mouth of God, when the commandments came down from the mountain.

In modern British and American politics, 'family values' would probably be the main means of restoring the lost centre, the divine authority. In many ways, 'the family' stakes the role of God in modern political discourse. This is where the old values are now written down in stone. Why is our way of life sacred after all? Because it is the expression of family values. All values emanate from this centre, the family. If anyone lives in such as way as to violate or threaten the family, then they are violating the sacred principle of society. But for Sartre, there is no such principle. Family values would simply be the latest attempt to smuggle the deity back into society – to select certain norms, certain lifestyles and endow them with an original force, as if they were inscribed in the heavens.

Abandonment: the Sartrean project

We have a thousand ways of talking to ourselves – individually and collectively – as if our lives had been dictated from outside. In all of this inner speech, we tell ourselves not just that we had to be like this, but that we ought to be like this. We had to go to war to defend ourselves: that is the instinct of survival. She can't live like that: it threatens the family and without the family, all will be chaos. I didn't choose this relationship: it was chosen for me, by my feelings – love at first sight or a meeting of souls.

Sartre does not deny the existence of passions or instincts. Indeed he is going to give them an important place in the next phase of his arguments in *EH*. But throughout the Sartrean project, he insists that what we call our instincts are not given to us from outside, by some external authority. At some deep level, I have chosen these instincts, these patterns of feeling. Nothing comes before my choices. These are not, of course, just ordinary choices. They are the choices of my inner being. But still, they are just as much my doing as the decisions that I am more conscious of having made. If I experience this overwhelming drive, jealousy say, that is because at some fundamental level I have chosen to be the sort of person who is open to such feelings. If it seemed to me in that moment that I had no choice but to shoot that intruder in self-defence, then that may have been true – but nothing other than I myself put that necessity at the heart of my being. I made myself that way. I was acting out a necessity that had no origin except in my own decisions.

> Sartrean Project: Fourth Existential Principle
> *I am alone with my decisions in the universe.*

Abandonment is our way of experiencing the world, not a theological deduction from a metaphysical chain of reasoning. Sartre believes that we actually experience the godlessness of the world in each moment of our lives. Godlessness is his way of describing the quality of experience. Indeed it is effectively the Sartrean definition of experience: this hanging in an empty space, this demand from the outside to be filled with substance, by my choices, of acts and of meanings.

In *The Reprieve*, Mathieu is standing on a bridge over the Seine. He has been thinking about the war to come. He should be joining his unit in the army. He looks out over the night and in that instant he also becomes acutely conscious of the physical texture of the world under his touch – the rough feel of the stone parapet. Surely this must be a significant moment, he reflects. Surely, this is history in the making: there must be a viewpoint out there from which the significance is apparent. But then he realizes there is no such exterior viewpoint. Even the great moments of history – or the most intense points of an individual's being – even those points are unwittnessed. They simply come into existence inside this endlessly empty space – that is our experience of the world. In other words, the world is never filled by our experience – we always have the feeling that even the greatest experiences have not quite filled the world. There remains a space, an emptiness surrounding them.

'I am free for nothing,' he reflected wearily. Not a sign in the sky, nor on the earth ...

'Nothing' is Sartre's other word for this emptiness that always surrounds our experience, even our greatest experience. The world expresses no interest:

... the things of the world were too utterly immersed in the war that was theirs, they turned their manifold heads towards the east.

We live amidst a clutter of objects, objects that take no interest in our goings on. It is their indifference that encloses us – and not the presence of a god for whom we count. This is abandonment – to live unregarded by the universe. Instead of God, things. Indifference, not concern. In the face of this indifference in things, I am abandoned to my own life, as I have made it.

This is the quality of experience that Sartre is trying to invoke in the passage about abandonment in *EH*. A shorthand compression, a crystallization of this strand in the Sartrean project.

To experience the world is to experience abandonment. As Sartre expresses the same idea in *Being and Nothingness*:

> *we appear to ourselves as having the character of an unjustifiable fact.*
>
> (*BN*, p.80)

He also offers an extraordinary image of the abandoned condition later in the work. He describes our consciousness as an explosion that we direct against a background of blank indifference:

> *as though against the length of an immense and monotonous wall of which it cannot see the end.*
>
> (*BN*, p.204)

In such a universe, religious faith appears to be an evasion of the quality of our experience, our inwardness, our dependence on our own 'interiority' (*BN*, p.232ff).

Abandonment: Sartre, Nietzsche and Heidegger

Sartre's announcement of abandonment has some roots in the work of the nineteenth-century German philosopher, Nietzsche, and particularly in his strange vision, *Thus Spake Zarathustra* (*TSZ*):

> *The saint answered: 'I make songs and sing them; and when I make songs, I laugh, cry, and hum; thus I praise God ...' But when Zarathustra was alone he spoke thus to his heart: 'Could it be possible? This old saint in the forest has not yet heard anything of this, that God is dead!'*
>
> (Nietzsche, *TSZ*, I, p.3)

There is also the continuing dialogue with Heidegger. The concept that corresponds most closely to Sartrean abandonment is Heidegger's notion of 'Being-in-the world' (*Being and Time*, p.91). In his extended reflections on this notion, Heidegger sees 'Worldhood' as a part of human reality. There is, it appears, no external creator; we make our own world. Indeed, for Heidegger, there is no conception of a world at all outside human experience. There would be things, objects and so on, but these only belong to a world from a human perspective. Heidegger consistently talks of how the world is a 'lit up' around human awareness.

There are some logical connections with Sartre. But the flavour is entirely different. There is a kind of religious feeling to Heidegger's treatment of 'Being-in-the-World', as he himself later argued. The radical atheism is a distinctively Sartrean feeling and not really a pre-given existential doctrine.

How to be free 4

AIMS

This chapter tells the next stage of the 'defence' of existentialism, or of the Sartrean project. Now Sartre encounters directly the charge that critical philosophy is a 'corrupter' of youth, a bad influence on the future of society.

* We examine his key example, for the whole text, the story of his own role as a teacher in giving advice to a student in a terrible dilemma during the years of the occupation: applied Sartreanism – the Sartrean project in its application. This extended example is presented by Sartre in terms of his key concepts and particularly the idea of 'abandonment'. But in this tale we are shown how what Sartre has now defined as 'existentialism', which seemed so negative in the preceding definition, comes to be a philosophy of freedom and even of liberation. Or, we might say, how the Sartrean project can take hold of experience – how Sartre can set you free!

* After looking at the story, we can define some key practical principles of the Sartrean project – principles of existential education and their relation to past thinkers.

* The chapter then concludes with the wider issue of the nature of education and advice in relation to individual freedom.

(This chapter covers the arguments corresponding to Methuen edition, pp.34–8.)

THE EMOTIONAL TURNING-POINT

In the first half of *EH*, Sartre has confronted his audience, and his readers, with a project defined in a hail of negatives, coming together to pinpoint our being on earth. Cumulatively, from 'existence' through 'responsibility' and 'anguish', to the whole state of 'abandonment', each concept has defined some limit or loss or absence in our lives. Though there is no God, and never was one, our being is still abandoned, or 'forlorn', through that absence. But at the start, Sartre's announced purpose was to *defend* an approach he has called 'existentialism' and specifically to refute the charge of inducing despair – to show that this is not the philosophy of defeatism which its opponents, on all sides, might claim. There is a certain growing suspense in *EH*: will he be able to turn such darkness into a source of light after all? Now, in the centre of the text and of the argument, he turns to the practical implications of his project.

We shall now see how in his central example, Sartre both reaches the darkest point, and begins to turn the argument round.

At the emotional centre of the *EH*, we find not an abstract step, but a concrete situation, a story in which Sartre himself features as one character. He suddenly introduces a little tale about a person who faces what it really means to be abandoned. It is also about the role of Sartre as a practical philosopher, an influence on the lives of others.

Abandonment and advice: a tale of two dilemmas

Sartre tells his audience, and his readers, that they are now going to have a story, one introduced as both 'an example' and 'a case'. What follows, implies Sartre, serves some other purpose, highlight some general meaning. Even that prelude suggests a more positive tone to his argument.

Sartre does not tell us in advance exactly what the message will be, except to say that we are about to witness 'the state of abandonment' as represented by the plight of one of his own students. This young man has no name in the story and neither do any of the other characters. He appears, when we encounter him, to be very far from abandoned in the usual sense, that is the sense of having been deserted, left to fend for himself, cast out into the world. On the contrary, he is, we would normally say, someone who is rather surrounded, even burdened, by other people. In fact, there seems to be a kind of upside-down quality to this 'example'. As we read it, we wonder who is the example of being abandoned, for the young man's problem seems to be precisely whether to *abandon* someone else.

Sartre now turns briefly, but vividly, into his novelist self. The young man is given a situation – a highly charged one. We begin in the family. He has a mother and a father, though there is, it is true, a problem in the family. His parents have separated and the young man is now with the mother. Here, then, is the first hint of an abandonment: the father has left. But from that point of view, it seems as if the truly abandoned person is the mother, if anyone: certainly the student seems to feel that way, for he experiences his situation precisely as the need to remedy her state of desertedness, of having been abandoned in the world.

There is already something suggestive about this story, since Sartre introduced his abstract definition of 'abandonment' by talking about the absence of the great father figure, God. He insisted there that we are all abandoned in the sense that no God watches over us. It seems that this young man experiences that condition more acutely because it has been repeated at a more local level, by the desertion of the father. The young man's problem is twofold: abandoned by the father, he also seeks to stand in for that missing figure, to fill his place.

THE SARTREAN PARABLE

The predicament (1)

Abandonment is the feeling of having to replace an absent father.

But there is also an historic situation. An enemy (the Germans) have occupied this person's country and in the war of 1940 his brother has been killed fighting in the defeated French army. The father then turns out to be a threefold 'abandoner'. Not only has he left the mother and the son: he is also in the process of abandoning his country. It seems that this father intends to collaborate, to go over to the enemy. In fact, that appears to be one of the reasons for the family dispute. This situation is created at every turn by the disappearance of the true father, morally as well as emotionally and indeed economically.

It seems significant that this lost father is presented as the reason why the young man has approached Sartre for advice. Various dilemmas have arisen because of this missing father, dilemmas which are presented to Sartre in the hope that he will give an answer. We have, therefore, a strong sense of the motive for seeking advice. Is Sartre not being asked to take the place of that father?

THE SARTREAN PARABLE

The predicament (2)

To be an adviser is to become a substitute for the lost father.

Being the young man's teacher, Sartre is being invited to fill the gap in his life, as he experiences it, to remedy the lack of an authority figure. The whole situation presents itself in the form of a lack, the loss of the true centre of authority.

Mother has been left on the son's hands and not only the mother: it feels as if the country too has been passed over by the father and left as a responsibility for the son. His real dilemma begins here. He could go and join the Free French forces in England or he could remain and support his mother in Nazi-occupied Paris. In both cases, he seems to be substituting for the missing father. In the family, he is taking on the role of carer. In the country, he is inheriting the role of defender. There is also a link: the dead brother.

Sartre says that the young man feels a naive but intense desire to exact retribution on behalf of his brother, which means that this is not simply a choice between family and country, between private and public allegiance. If he does not join the Free French forces, then he is also choosing not to take vengeance for his brother.

The young man has a dilemma and Sartre really rubs in its painful intensity. On one side, he is said to realize that his mother depends entirely on him, materially and also psychologically. He has taken on a role as the purpose of life for this woman. If he leaves her, she will be truly abandoned. By his presence, he is keeping her alive, in several senses. On the other side, if he does not go he can be said to be abandoning his country and also the memory of his brother. In both of these roles, the student would be taking on the father's role, trying to fill gaps left by his various betrayals. In this sense, the young man's plight is a metaphor for the situation of all human beings.

> THE SARTREAN PARABLE
>
> *Ways forward (1)*
>
> **To live one's abandonment means to try to fill the gap left by the absent father: this is impossible, but inescapable.**

In his abstract definition, Sartre said that to understand abandonment and his version of existentialism as a whole, means to think through to the end the full consequence of the absence of God. Now we have a story about a man who faces in his own life the impossible task of taking on the roles left behind by a lost father figure. It seems as if all his dilemmas originate in this one loss. The story, therefore, is brilliantly chosen to convey what for Sartre is the widest meaning of existential 'abandonment'. Here we have the key example of the coherence of his personal project and its contribution to modern thought generally, as the expression of a novelist-philosopher.

There is clearly both a philosophical and a psychological meaning to this story, which is perhaps why Sartre introduces it as both an 'example' and a 'case'. Philosophically, the young man represents the human condition: he encounters the world in terms of a missing centre of authority. Psychologically, the point seems to be that though we are all in that position, all the time, since God is the real absence, there are moments in our lives when we really experience that abandonment in practice. Seen from Sartre's point of view, the story is a metaphor for the human lot. For the young man, it is an actual experience of that condition. The implication is that most of the time, we do not actually notice our abandonment.

> THE SARTREAN PARABLE
>
> *Ways forward (2)*
>
> **Painful dilemmas are our way of actively encountering the state of abandonment.**

What is to be done? Applied Sartrean ethics

Sartre explores the dilemma and the more he writes, the worse the situation sounds. First, the young man realizes that his duty to the mother and to the country are really not the same kind of thing. In his mother's case, whatever he does will definitely have an immediate benefit. He will certainly be doing good, in so far as he stays with her. She will find her life more bearable in all kinds of ways. On the other hand, if he chooses his country, then it is not clear what effect that choice will have. For one thing, he may never make it to the Free French base in England. He may only get as far as a useless camp in Spain. And then when he arrives, he may not find anything useful to do. He may just spend his time doing little bits of administration. No one can be sure of his effect on the war, whereas the young man feels – and Sartre seems to agree – that he can be certain of his effect in the family.

Sartre says that this dilemma is truly impossible. The choice isn't really coherent. The two options are simply too different from each other for the young man to be able even to compare them properly. It isn't like choosing between two careers or two relationships or two political parties. The possibilities come from alien worlds. Finally, at rock bottom, where philosophy comes down to earth, or recognizes that that is where it always was, both the student and the teacher have to face the fact that if there is no God, there is also no answer. Is this, then, defeatism after all? That too depends on how you look at it:

KEY QUOTE

If values are uncertain, if they are still too abstract to determine the particular, concrete case under consideration, nothing remains but to trust our instincts.

(Methien edn, p.36)

This is really the heart of the idea of abandonment, as represented in this story, this example and case. We are abandoned by God, which means, in practice, that there is no universal or uniform code of values by which we can live our lives. You can see this situation in two ways, and it is on this ambiguity that the emotional tone of the argument turns.

Within this parable, there unfolds the central argument of the Sartrean project as a whole:

**The Sartrean Project: From Abandonment to Commitment –
A Double Argument**

To be abandoned means to have no God.

To have no God means to have no firm or fixed values.

All values are partial and our dilemmas have no answer.

We are trapped in   We are free agents.
our dilemmas.

In this distinctively Sartrean argument, the fact that some of our personal dilemmas are truly impossible is the sign, in each of our lives, that we are abandoned and also that we are free. If there were a God, he would have given us at least a clear value by which to make such decisions. In fact, for Sartre, we can tell that there is no God in our lives by the way in which we face such insoluble choices. The insolubility is a sign of our forlornness and also a mark of our freedom.

What about Sartre's own role? What should he advise? The key point is that the adviser is in exactly the same boat as the seeker of advice. He has no access to any Truth, any firm value which can solve the problem. He cannot point to a sacred text and say: look, there is our answer. There is no God whose mouthpiece he can be on earth. Not only that; there is no human philosophy which can take the problem out of the student's own hands. For example, Kant says that one should never treat another person as a means instead of an end. Good, says Sartre. But what does that mean in this specific case? If he leaves his mother, he may be said to treat her as a means, to the end of serving a higher cause. But if he stays, he will be treating the others who do the fighting as a means, helping him to fulfil his personal choice of family duty and affection. The adviser, too, faces the existential fact that there is no outside answer: he too carries the burden of human freedom.

Even the idea of 'trusting our instincts' is, of course, only what we make of it. Sartre goes on to show that when the young man tries to decide what he really feels, he again faces an active choice. Does he feel more about his mother than about his country? At present, he is still at home. So it seems as if his feelings lie in that direction. On the other hand, maybe he only seems to feel that way because he has not yet left. Maybe if he took the other path, his feelings of the need to act would find expression and turn out to be stronger. This is an example of Sartre's wider, and rather strange-looking idea, that we are responsible not just for what we do, but also for what we feel. It is another self-deception to think that feelings will rescue us from our freedom or our forlornness. We make the space within which our feelings find expression, or remain suppressed, by the decisions which we ourselves have taken.

How about the act of seeking advice? Might that at least not be a way of reducing both our abandonment and the burden of our individual freedom? Here Sartre concludes his example by pointing out that people choose the advisers whom they then try to follow. If the young man had gone to a priest he would have been seeking different advice. Even then, there are different priests, some sympathetic to the occupation and others active in the French Resistance.

Sartre gives the story no ending, either as a narrator or as an adviser. He never tells the student how to act and he does not tell us what happened. In fact, the tone, though, suggests that the decision has already been made and the contrast between Sartre and the priests and between the collaborationist and resistant priests, weights the whole case towards the choice of the Free French army. We aren't told, but it feels as if a choice has been made. As readers, or listeners, we too are in the same boat: we have to trust our instincts. It is we who must decide the outcome of the story and we must also decide on the emotional significance. We can make this into a tale of someone trapped or into a tale of a man realizing his freedom.

Sartrean practical principles

The story confronts us with an 'example' which never yields a simple message. That is part of Sartre's point: logic and theory finally stop short in the face of a person in a specific situation. You are never going to come up with a philosophy that can absorb a moment from a concrete life and turn it into an idea.

However, we have through this tale come to appreciate more about two important questions and to grasp at least some of their significance. The first is 'abandonment', as seen in the crisis of the student who must decide his own future between irreconcilable alternatives and values. This crisis is the darkest moment in *EH* and also the emotional turning-point.

First question: What does it mean to be abandoned?

Negative response: To lack the father, the outside authority.

Affirmative response: To face one's own freedom.

Sartre also places this student as someone who has come to him for help, for advice. He is a person in a dilemma and also in pursuit of counsel. From that point of view, this young man is a representative of many in the audience or reading the text of the lecture: Sartre is faced by a world which needs advice, which is listening to him in the hope of receiving an answer to its questions, a hint as to how it should live now. So the story has, at least, a double question. It is an example of some sort of plight, as experienced by the student. But it is also an *example* of Sartre's own plight, as an adviser, as the hoped-for source of wisdom. Though the story does not deliver exactly a moral about this role of adviser, there is a practical principle, with a positive aspect:

Second question: **What does it mean to give advice?**

Negative response: **The adviser is called upon to fill the gap created by the absent father, the lost authority.**

Affirmative response: **To give true advice is to refuse to fill that gap, but rather to return the seeker to his or her own freedom.**

The negative and positive aspects are finely balanced in every aspect of the story. Having said that Sartre shows himself refusing to give what would normally be regarded as advice, one can also see this as precisely an example of how to advise others. Probably the best term for this approach to advising would be 'sincerity' or, in the idiom of Sartre's wider philosophy, 'good faith'.

At the heart of the Sartrean project as crystallized around *EH* is an educative commitment, educative in the widest sense:

Sartrean Project: The Educative Principle
Never advise a person in such a way as to disguise their freedom from them. To do so is to teach insincerity or bad faith.

This means in practice never encouraging a person to look at his or her own life as if they were not a free agent. To do so would be to live insincerely or in 'bad faith'. There is a link between advice and living more generally. It seems likely that a person who lives without sincerity or, as Sartre's *Being and Nothingness* would say, in 'bad faith' teaches bad faith to others; one who lives sincerely and in good faith teaches good faith to others.

SARTRE'S OTHERS

The Socratic project

In our account of the opening of *EH*, we looked at the implied relation between Sartre and Plato's figure of the embattled Socrates, the symbol of beleaguered philosophy. This parable also has profound links with the Socratic idea. In the *Apology*, Socrates confronts the charge that he gives unwanted advice:

> *It may seem curious to you that I should go around giving advice like this and busying myself in people's private affairs ...*

Socratic advice is suspect because it does not deliver easy answers – and just so, Sartrean advice delivers the advisee back into his own freedom, his own dilemmas. Sartrean wisdom, like Socratic wisdom, aims to asks questions that restore the freshness – and the painfulness – of the person's freedom. This style of advice was seen as corrupting – and Socrates dies at the end of the *Apology*, drinking the poisoned draught of hemlock allocated by the orthodox court. Sartre's central parable is, therefore, a way of linking his ideas with this deep tradition in western thought – and with its ancient scandal.

Heidegger's care

Sartre's scene of advice is also closely involved with the more immediately preceding ideas of Heidegger. In *Being and Time* (p.158) there is a powerful discussion of what is called 'solicitude', concern for others. Heidegger distinguishes between 'two extreme possibilities'. Solicitude 'can, as it were, take away "care" from the Other', 'it can *leap in* for him'. Such concern is the kind that takes the other's life out of his own reach – giving answers from outside: 'In such solicitude the Other can become one who is dominated and dependent.' By contrast, there is also the possibility of a kind of solicitude 'which does not so much leap in for the Other as *leap ahead* of him'. The aim now is 'not ... to take away his "care" but rather ... to give it back to him authentically as such for the first time'. This is closely related to the concern shown by Sartre for his pupil: he tries to give the young man back his problem, as a choice to be made only by himself.

But there is, as throughout, a deeper contrast between the Sartrean vision and Heidegger. Above all, Heidegger has an ideal of true 'understanding':

> **Only he who already understands can listen.**
>
> (Heidegger, *Being and Time*, p.208)

Sartre does not suggest any such moment of real understanding: the other remains more distant and difficult, more opaque. In addition, there is in Sartre a focus on taking actions, which goes beyond the more contemplative aura of Heidegger's discussion.

Summary

At the centre of *EH*, then, Sartre makes a concrete case for his personal version of an approach which might be termed Socratic as much as existential. In the next chapter, we shall see how through the second half of this great work, Sartre takes up this challenge of giving humane encouragement without fostering any illusions, as he has tried to do in the case of the abandoned young man.

5 How to be a person

AIMS

* This chapter presents the 'humanist' phase of the unfolding argument where Sartre comes to define the *value* of being human.

* Four concepts are central to his evolving case: the self; the dignity of man; the human condition; true or full humanity.

We examine each concept in turn, looking at the way Sartre is reducing a potentially grandiose ideal to the most basic expression possible – a distinctively Sartrean humanism.

Then we look at Sartrean humanism as an Art of the Good Life.

(This chapter covers the arguments corresponding to Methuen edition, pp. 40–56.)

Preparing the humanist turn

In the next phase of *EH*, the central concept is humanism – now Sartre has to make good the unexpected part of his title. The turn to 'humanism' is a recognition of the fact that the Sartrean project cannot be accounted for only in terms of a take on 'existentialism' – there has to be another term to articulate a more affirmative impulse. This is the most audacious move of all.

But first, preparing the way for his affirmation, Sartre inevitably swings into the sharpest downward spiral of the whole address – inevitably, because that is the inner logic of the Sartrean project. He cannot afford to risk the positive until he has reconfirmed the negative and in the darkest possible way. So we have the encounter with fascism.

The fascists have been defeated, as of 1945. In fact they were driven from France in August 1944. But fascism still remains a human possibility – one of the ways that humanity could choose to be. Consider the Sartrean principles – especially that of anguish. The future is always open to us. Our decisions tomorrow will count just as much as those of yesterday. Then if, Sartre continues, a new generation comes into being and it chooses to reconnect itself to that now defeated possibility, to fascism – what then? Then fascism may win – and in that case, given time, the fascist vision may work itself into the texture of experience. Finally we may wind up living in a fascist world.

KEY QUOTE

If so, Fascism will then be the truth of man.

(Methuen edn, p.40)

Anatomy of key quote

- *The human is not made from outside but from within.*
- *Whatever we make of ourselves, that becomes humanity.*
- *We have no criterion outside history with which to judge history. If we make a world where cruelty is the norm, then we cannot judge that world by some abstract standard of human nature.*

We cannot say: this fascist world is a failed version of being human, by some fixed standard of the human. Not that we have to accept whatever the world is. Sartre is saying the opposite of that. But we have to *make* a different world, our own chosen alternative. So if you don't want to live in a world where it is human to be fascist, then you have to set about making a different world. In this respect, Sartrean existentialism is a call to action, an activist philosophy – even an anti-philosophy.

Having summoned the ghost to the feast, Sartre can then make the leap – risk the most affirmative formulation of his Sartrean project. Indeed, in a way it is the only attempt at a semi-systematic declaration of a positive outlook.

Now we come to the four points of recrystallization of the Sartrean project as humanism.

THE SELF

It is deeply rooted in the whole Sartrean personality that the approach to the human is first an approach to the self.

> ### Sartrean project: First Humanist Principle
> *I can never stand outside my 'self'.*

Sartre points back to his philosophical ancestor, Descartes here: 'I think, therefore I am'. It is not the 'think' that interests Sartre, though, but the 'I am'. Nothing comes before the 'I am'. To become conscious is to experience this sense of 'I am', of individual being. Consciousness is always an expression of this original experience. Every one of my ideas has within it this sense of 'I am-ness'.

Sartre is not just talking about the moments of conscious introspection. He is saying that every one of my thoughts has within it this 'I am'. I may be thinking about the world out there, about politics, the football results or the weather, but my ideas will always have this 'I am' inside them. To think is to express this feeling of personal being.

We have no way of experiencing the world without this 'I am' at its centre. Here Sartre commits himself to a recognition of the strength of this 'self' – we do have somewhere to start from, in our constant struggle to reconstruct our worlds, a struggle that in 1945 has become momentarily also an historic task.

Nothing but death can destroy the self. The self sticks to all possible experience.

In some ways, this seems now to be the most dated of Sartre's arguments. When he does defend it, he is mainly concerned to argue against what he presents as Marxist objections – the view that existentialists are just bourgeois individualists, dressed up as radicals. But from a later perspective, there seem to be lots of other arguments against this approach. Sartre seems to think that any attempt to get 'behind' the self must smuggle back some hidden essence – human nature, instinct, God. In fact, we could find a different way of thinking about the 'I am'. We could, in particular, put more emphasis on the role of language in the shaping of human experience. We could see 'I am' not as a fixed starting point, but as itself the construct of language.

We have this experience, of 'I am', as beings participating in language. It is language that puts the 'I' at the centre of my consciousness. You cannot, in this view, separate the experience of 'I am' from the word 'I'. But language is social, not personal. I become an 'I am' only by entering into language. Before language, in the world of the baby, there is no 'I am' – only a far more diffuse relation to the world. So Sartre might be said to create a false distinction between self and society – by setting aside the domain of language. There is no 'I' who learns language – the 'I' only comes into existence within language. The 'self' is linguistic construct. As we will see, Heidegger responded with a criticism along these lines.

These arguments have probably done most to shift the Sartrean project from the centre of modern discussion about identity and politics. It is this focus on 'the self', outside and before language, that has made Sartre's approach seem in retrospect more conservative than radical. Against the unitary Sartrean self have been ranged the radicalism of deconstruction and post-structuralism and also of more modern forms of psychoanalysis and feminism. But it is important to recapture the full force of the Sartrean project within which this sense of self emerged. Sartre is not simply fabricating a positive formula for the occasion. He is drawing together ideas and images that are deeply embedded in his imaginative development.

For example, in *The Age of Reason*, Mathieu reaches a crisis – he feels his established life coming to an end, something else is starting. In that moment, he recognizes the tenacity of the self: a centre that is 'beyond analysis'. What is this self? First it is 'an ancient habit' – which sounds mechanical. But actually this habit is a habitual way of choosing – of choosing to be this person, right down to the details of what he eats, how he dresses and even where he turns to look at a given minute.

This is an extraordinary vision – of a self that is everywhere present, but present as a kind of ground of freedom. Every grain in experience expresses the choices of the self. If I look at that tree over there, outside the door, then I am expressing the inner principle of my self. Here Sartre is truly challenging the Freudian idea of the unconscious. Far from being unwittingly conservative, this is perhaps the most philosophically radical point in *EH*. Sartre is the thinker who comes closest to offering an alternative to the rising orthodoxy of the unconscious as a way of thinking about how our lives extend beyond our reach, into areas below, behind us. For Sartre, this hidden realm is not the unconscious, but the self:

> *He relaxed his grip and let it go: all this happened deep in his inmost self, in a region where words possess no meaning.*

Sartre seems outdated if he is taken as the last big defender of the crystalline self – the last would-be radical to believe in the old western self. In that kind of interpretation, he sounds more like a certain kind of old-fashioned liberal – or even conservative. But, when you take the Sartrean project as a whole, Sartre has a very strange model of the self. It is not at all a daylight principle. The Sartrean self is a fundamental core of continuous choosing – one which is truly my own, my responsibility – yet it is beyond words and as deeply within or below as any Freudian unconscious. Sartre's self is rational but not conscious in a simple way. The self is a name for the deep rationality beneath or before or beyond ordinary awareness. I have already chosen before I awaken to my choices. The challenge then is to recognize that original freedom.

THE DIGNITY OF MAN

The dignity of man: this kind of claim does not seem very distinctive, on the face of it! Most philosophies and ideologies claim to promote human dignity. For example, in modern politics:

* The **religious conservatives** see themselves as defenders of human dignity – meaning proper values, according to the old authority. The dignity of man means respect for the traditional way of life. It also means recognition of the soul and the relation to God.

* Whereas for **liberals**, human dignity means recognition of the rights of the individual, freedom from humiliation or oppression.

In the Sartrean project, as crystallized in this humanist form, human dignity has a very specific meaning. Our dignity consists in the full recognition that we are not objects. This recognition begins, in the first place, as self-recognition, self-affirmation. All around me, there are objects: tables, rocks, trees. I affirm my own human dignity by seeing the distinction between my mode of being and that of all these various objects. My existence has this distinctive inwardness, the world starts from inside me.

> Sartrean Project: Second Humanist Principle
> *Dignity is inwardness.*

But in recognizing my own dignity, I instantly come to recognize that of others. I have not really grasped my own inwardness unless I see that other people also possess the same depth. Just as the world springs into being from inside me, so it rises up from inside each of the others. Each of us has this experience of the world continuously springing up from our inward centre. I have not grasped my own freedom if I do not see everyone else as possessing an equivalent.

You could call it reciprocity – this sense of equivalent inwardness in each of the others. Someone who fails to make this recognition of the others has also failed to grasp her or his own human dignity. You cannot recognize yourself as a person without simultaneously recognizing the others. This means that there can be no half-recognition of the dignity of humanity. You cannot stop at a certain point, draw the line and say: I will recognize the human inwardness of those people, but there it stops. Yet this is one of the most common ways of arguing or thinking in modern politics and culture.

Take the case of 'ethnic' conflict. I will recognize the dignity of all the others, except 'them' – except the Catholics or the Jews, the Albanians or the Palestinians. They are returned to the sphere of the objective – the objects. They are not allowed the dignity of the rest of us – they are not seen as centres of the world, but only as objects within the world as defined by us. You can also see sexism in these terms: a misogynistic denial of the creative inwardness of women, seeing women as objects.

You can in no way say that this humanism is an afterthought – this goes right back into the Sartrean project – which is continuously committed to an equivalent defence of the dignity of man. But this is the moment when Sartre has the courage to leap into an affirmative representation.

In Sartre's fiction, he imagines the denial of the dignity of man, with despairing vividness. Here is Mathieu, looking over the doomed city of Paris (*The Reprieve*):

> *Dormitory-refectories for those about to be mobilized. Their ultimate purpose could already be surmised: they would become 'strategic points', and, in the end, targets. ... A new world was coming into being: the austere and practical world of functional objects.*

War is the most systematic expression of the denial of human dignity. It is also the culmination of the modern state as a vehicle for the denial of human dignity. For the state, individuals are simply functional entities – they are objects to be rearranged so that they can be employed in the most efficient possible way.

In *Being and Nothingness*, Sartre sees a dignity implied by the nature of consciousness itself. My awareness of my own existence, from within excludes 'all objectivity' (*BN*, p.241). There is no way I can 'conceive of my existence in the form of an object'. I have no power to turn myself into an object, in my own eyes. However I choose to live, as brutalized as the world around me becomes or is made, I cannot experience that world except through my self and I cannot recognize that self without reigniting the flicker of a central inwardness.

Sartre does not think true alienation is conceivable ... outside death ... I can never lose this inward relation to myself. Total alienation would mean that I lost that depth and encountered myself as a pure object, over there, in the world, outside my control and also beyond my understanding. Such alienation would define, for Sartre, the stripping away of the dignity that is implicit in being human. Alienation has become a modern orthodoxy – here again Sartrean humanism is at odds with what became the more radical aspects of modern thought.

Sartre's sense of human dignity is also part of his atheism. For Sartre, to be a humanist means embracing atheism without reservation. The concept of God is, in the Sartrean project, a reduction of the dignity of man. Here again *EH* is a concentrated expression of a long-standing commitment. In *Being and Nothingness* (p.290) Sartre sees the idea of the relation to God and a negation of humanness – whereas in many previous forms of humanism, the relation to God was part of the dignity of the human (e.g. Renaissance humanism). Sartre sees man standing before God – over there is the being for whom I can at last be reduced to a pure object – seen in the round, from outside. But God can never be reduced to an object – I have no answering perspective on that Being. The effect, concludes Sartre, would be one of pure 'shame': 'This is shame before God.'

If there were a God, I would encounter him in pure 'object-ness' – he would know me entirely from the outside, God is, in the terms of the Sartrean project, a denial of the need for human inwardness. If there were a God that would mean there would be a point of view in the universe from which I could be entirely understood from the outside, as an object of the knowledge of an other. Sartre is affronted by this idea. In fact, he clearly believes it belongs to a fantasy of shame and a kind of wish to be abased before the power of the other.

In *EH* Sartre insists that dignity is reciprocal. I recognize my own depth, the freedom that comes from inwardness and in the same moment I must recognize the depth of other people. This argument has a long history in Sartre – and behind it is the notion of God as the exception. He could recognize his inwardness without any reciprocity – and he could comprehend me without any sense of my inwardness. That is why, in the Sartrean project, human dignity goes with a radically atheist version of humanism.

Sartre's principle of human dignity also emerges from his approach to love and sexuality. Through Sartre's philosophy and fiction, there runs a series of images of false love – entrapping, denying, reductive encounters under the sign of romance or love or sex. These all share a principle – a negative principle – the negation of human dignity, meaning inwardness with oneself. In *Being and Nothingness* (p.374) there is a vivid reflection on the mechanics of seduction. If the 'Other' attempts to seduce me by taking on the quality of a pure 'object', an 'object state', then I am denied the chance to recognize her or his dignity. I can only enter into 'relation' with an object as something I want to possess. My desire is aroused only in the shape of an urge to own, to possess. This is the inhumanity of desire – and it is seduction as negation of human dignity, the other face of torture, as seen above.

The extreme case is masochism. Here, says Sartre, I try to treat myself as an object – dedicated entirely to the pleasure of the other. My being is transformed – hollowed out from within. This is the most self-negating response to my own inwardness (*BN*, p.378): 'Finally I project being nothing more than an object.' But there is a paradox to masochism. It is not really about the presentation of myself to the other person. In truth, the masochist is fascinated with his or her own object-ness.

This second humanist principle, of dignity, therefore, has deep roots in the Sartrean project. It is not fair, as is sometimes claimed, to see Sartre as improving a humanist face to make his ideas more acceptable. What is true is that he is turning certain long-standing thoughts and images round – so that they appear in their more affirmative character. These humanist principles are affirmative recrystallizations of deep motives and consistent orientations.

THE HUMAN CONDITION

The third humanist principle is less obviously affirmative. It is the assertion that we share common limits. Yet in its way this is an even more affirmative position.

> Sartrean Project: Third Humanist Principle
> *Our shared limits are our common ground.*

Sartre began his argument by rejecting any human essence. But now he wants to insist that there is a human common ground. What can we have in common, if we do not share human nature or a human soul? Sartre accepts the common reality of a human condition. But he immediately insists that this condition is not to be defined in any fixed terms. What we have in common is that we make our choices within a certain sense of limits. We can have no idea of what it would mean to make choices without some sense of limits. The human condition is simply this ineradicable sense of choosing within limits.

We do not know what choosing would mean, argues Sartre, without the shared limit of mortality. Indeed, it seems that without mortality we would not really have the human experience of choosing, of deciding on our own being or our own actions. Everything would be reversible, somewhere further down the road. Mortality is experienced differently, for the prisoner in a camp and a man in a leafy suburb. But they still have the basis for a common condition – their choices are situated and their situation includes mortality.

By the human condition, Sartre means the potential for empathy. I, in my suburb, can make some attempt to imagine her, in her camp – and vice versa. There is no fixed human nature to enable us to understand one another's experience. But there is a springboard from which to leap.

Here Sartre is trying to turn around the core of the preceding existential arguments. In denying a fixed human essence, he seemed to leave the way open for a kind of atomized vision: no shared humanity, no common ground. All empathy would be self-deception, delusion. It would never be possible truly to recognize another's experience. There is, from Sartre's perspective, something in that – a core of inwardness that can only be accessed by the self. Yet in another way, he does preserve or reassert a basis for common humanity – in these shared limits.

The limits cannot be defined in the abstract. There is no stateable list of universal limits. Sartre is not thinking about the inability to fly or breathe under water. He has in mind something more emotional or even spiritual. Within our sense of freedom, there is always an aspect of limitation – I make my choices on the ground of constraint. As I choose, I recognize that I am in this particular situation, with these options and not those. That is what choosing means, for human beings.

This distinctive idea of limits also goes deep into the wider Sartrean project. Here I am, making a choice. Let's say I am choosing whether to join my unit of the army, as Mathieu must in *The Reprieve*. There are, says Sartre in *Being and Nothingness*, 'causes' for this situation, certainly – the wider world factors, plus being born a bourgeois man in France and then having chosen this job not that, down to the fine grain of daily detail – being reasonably healthy, being listed on various documents. But these causes cannot be said directly to determine my choices. They enter into my choices only through my awareness of them – for Sartre:

> I am conscious of the causes which inspire my action.
>
> (*BN*, p.439)

I will never be able to blame the causes for my decision. I am in a situation, yes, but that is where my freedom surges up before me, into the world. What I cannot choose is ceasing to be responsible. I cannot choose to renounce the decision itself – another one will simply rise and take its place. So I encounter the limits of my life as choices, as decisions that challenge me to assert my freedom. This is the shared limit that makes our human condition: that we can have no experience of our specific situations, apart from our sense of being free and responsible.

> Freedom is total and infinite, which does not mean that it has no limits but that it never encounters them. The only limits which freedom bumps up against at each moment are those which it imposes on itself ...
>
> (*BN*, p.531)

It is my choosing which constructs or adopts the limits of my situation. In *Being and Nothingness*, this remains true even under torture. Sartrean humanism's third principle is the crystallization of a deep-rooted reflection on how common humanity can be reconciled with individual freedom. Our common humanity lies in this inescapable experience of 'situated freedom'.

FULL HUMANITY

Sartre comes to the pay-off – the affirmation that follows from all the negations, the value that is the outcome of all the criticism and denial. What is it that can stand in the face of human suffering, truly recognized? Is there really a humanist affirmation that does not in some way down play the facts of suffering and horror that constitute human history?

> Sartrean Project: Fourth Humanist Principle: The Leap
> *We create the absolute in a moment.*

Here I am, in my particular situation. It may be a dramatic predicament: I am a soldier, ordered to open fire. Or it may be more mundane: I open my arms, to give an embrace. Or I open my mouth, words form and I am on the point of replying to an invitation or an argument. In each case, Sartre argues, if I truly recognize my situation, I face a moment of absolute decision. If I fire the gun, I have chosen to become the person for whom that was the destined action. If I give the embrace, my life has expressed itself in that act of love or comfort. If I utter those words, they become the expression of a life: I am now the person who could say and stand by those words. To act in full consciousness of this truth is an awesome requirement. It involves what Sartre calls 'absolute commitment'.

The commitment is not just personal. If I open fire, I am committing myself to a version of humanity, in which people act like that. If I give the embrace, I have chosen to make humanity include that response: I have shown that being human now includes shooting or holding. I have committed not just myself, but everyone else to that version of humanity.

Conventional politics, following Sartre's arguments, is the means by which a society evades the demands of its own freedom. We have our way of life – the American way of life, the British character, the Islamic tradition, the Serbian spirit – and we act to preserve it. But people thereby evade the depth of their own responsibility.

Through the Sartrean project there is woven a skein of images of this total commitment – always paradoxical, the limit of what we can rationally comprehend. Here Sartrean rationalism touches its other shore. In *Being and Nothingness* (p.246) he has been analyzing grimly and relentlessly all the ways of evading the true self. These make up, according to Sartre, the fabric of everyday life and social convention, including conventional moral values. How can I recover my true self? How can I be what I am? 'I shall be my own authenticity', he declares, only by a moment of daring. I hear the 'call of conscience' – this is different from everyday morality. Ordinary moral values are a substitute for individual conscience. They are accessed just by asking: what does everyone else think about this? What would a normal person do now? But conscience is isolated – what would I think here? Conscience does not give a formulaic answer. On the contrary: if I respond to my own inner voice, then I take a leap into an uncharted world, my own individual future:

> **KEY CONCEPT**
>
> *Existential humanism*: the full recognition of this burden, the weight of commitment. Most of the time, we turn aside from such recognition, according to Sartre. We see ourselves as acting according to some external rules, norms or regulations. 'I had to ... that is our way of life ... this is how we do things ... those are the values ...'

> I launch out toward death with a resolute-decision as toward my own most peculiar possibility.
>
> (*BN*, p.246)

This seems to be an image of extreme separation, isolation. In fact, for Sartre, it is in this moment of commitment that I recover a true connection with the others:

> At this moment I reveal myself to myself in authenticity, and I
> raise others along with myself toward the authentic.

I take my own personal decision here and now. But that is precisely
what every other person is capable of – in their own individual
situations. By my example, I recall them to their possibility. This is
the possibility that we truly have in common, because it is our
possibility as human beings.

In this fourth humanist principle, the Sartrean project takes over a
language often associated with religious experience – 'revelation',
'unto-death', 'raises others'.

This humanism can indeed read itself back into the philosophy of
Sartre's predecessor, Søren Kierkegaard, who counts for Sartre as an
existentialist but also a Christian. Kierkegaard had a conception of
an ideal type, a knight of faith, who makes a kind of absolute
commitment to God that is seen as being like the leap of a dancer:

> It is supposed to be the most difficult task for a dancer to leap
> into a definite posture in such a way that there is no a second
> when he is grasping after the posture, but by the leap itself he
> stands fixed in that posture. Perhaps no dancer can do it – that
> is what the knight does.
>
> (Kierkegaard, *Fear and Trembling*, p.32)

Even at his most affirmative, Sartre also has negative applications in
mind. The other side of the coin in *EH* is that this armoury of
humanist concepts could be used to condemn those who are not
honest about their condition or who deny their own dignity or that
of others. The Sartrean ideal of commitment would find most of us
wanting, surely, most of our lives. In the wider Sartrean project, the
obverse of absolute commitment is bad faith and that would be the
status of much ordinary conduct and consciousness (*BN*, p.57).

EXISTENTIAL HUMANISM

A Sartrean 'art' of the good life

Sartre has set out his vision of his own personal humanism, deeply rooted in his previous thinking. He now builds on the closing notion of 'existential humanism'. Creativity emerges as the last – and the first – resort of hope.

Sartre finally tries to define further his notion of absolute commitment. He makes a metaphorical leap and compares morality with art. His example of the artist is very specific: Picasso, the modernist, the experimental hero, the avant-garde radical. According to Sartre, we face our moral lives as Picasso faces his canvas. Nothing is there in advance. Picasso is not following a pattern when he begins to paint. He makes movements over the surface. The lines appear. No previous decision predetermines the next movement of the brush. The picture is finished when he decides it is complete: the last line is the one he chooses as the end.

But, people said then of Picasso, and say now of other artists, by what right does he claim that is art? Who gave him the authority to say that that image was art? Modern news parallels. The controversy has not really gone away. Take the pile of bricks on the floor of the London Tate Gallery: who gave Carl Andre the authority to say that those bricks would be art? And why that number of bricks, rather than some other? Or take Tracey Emin's notorious unmade bed. The British artist Tracey Emin exhibited a dishevelled and unmade bed with lots of debris of a life – personal, intimate debris, the waste products of a particular experience. How could she say that was art? By what right did Tracy Emin thrust her bed into the public domain and give it the status of art? Why can't I do the same?

Sartre's reply would be: you do the same, all the time.

Sartrean Creativity
Morality is the most experimental art form.

For Sartre, the situation of the avant-garde artist is representative – and representative of our moral predicament. Morality does not exist outside our specific choices. Picasso brings the concept of art into the world within his specific painting. Tracey Emin is not only creating a specific work of art – she is taking responsibility for the concept of art as a whole. She is saying what art means for everyone else as well. We are all avant-garde artists when we make moral decisions. Morality becomes whatever is implicit in this specific choice. We all share:

KEY QUOTE
the same creative situation.
(Methuen edn, p.49)

Picasso does not just create a specific work of art – he also, in doing so, creates the values by which that work demands to be judged. The same is true of our moral choices.

Then Sartre comes to the notion of 'community'. This is one of the most influential ideas in contemporary politics and morality, on different sides of the political and moral spectrum, from 'radical' to 'conservative', liberal to fundamentalist. Community is not just a sociological idea, it is an ethical value. To act on behalf of the good of the community. To act in defence of the community. To preserve or uphold the community. It is the image of authenticity in contemporary arguments. Community is the antidote to selfishness. For radicals, it is the alternative to globalization. For conservatives, it is the repository of tradition and good old-fashioned values.

Sartre thinks of community differently:

> ## KEY QUOTE
> *but if I have excluded God the father, there must be somebody to invent values ... there is a possibility of creating a human community.*
>
> (Methuen edn, p.54)

Anatomy of key quote

- *Community is the outcome of my personal choices and those of all the others.*

- *Community is therefore universal – the human community.*

- *Community is the existential alternative to God – the common ground.*

- *Community for Sartre is not-yet. Community is the awaited outcome of all our moments of authentic and absolute commitment.*

In his finale, Sartre gives two examples of the invention of human community – literary examples. Maggie Tulliver from George Eliot's *Mill on the Floss* and La Sanseverina from Stendhal's *Charterhouse of Parma*. Maggie sacrifices herself for the good of society – and gives up the man she loves. This would be repugnant to La Sanseverina, who would sacrifice other people to the fulfilment of a true passion. Sartre does not see one as right, the other as wrong. He sees both as types of the commitment from which a human community may grow.

> ### Sartrean Creativity
> *Only an authentic individual can found a community.*

6 The aftermath

AIMS

✻ In this chapter, we look at the after-effects of *EH*, mainly focusing on Heidegger's 'Letter on Humanism', a direct response that is also a significant moment in modern philosophy.

✻ Finally, we look briefly at Sartre's future.

HEIDEGGER'S RESPONSE

As we saw in our introduction, in the aftermath of *EH* Sartre's influence was at its zenith. But already, in that moment, the reactions were setting in. In Paris, we saw how Camus refused to accept the Sartrean version of existentialism. Though she is more subtle and oblique in her escape, Simone de Beauvoir began in those same years to work on her feminist project, which became *The Second Sex* (1949) – another radical alternative for a post-war world.

But the most profound response came from Heidegger, the thinker with whom the fabric of *EH* is already in an intense dialogue. In the aftermath of Sartre's address, an anxious French correspondent wrote to Heidegger himself with a question. Here is the start of the reply:

---

you ask: How can we restore meaning to the word 'humanism'?

('Letter on humanism', in Heidegger's *Basic Writings*)

The reply became Heidegger's most deliberately accessible statement of his own position, his 'Letter on humanism'. It is to this argument that we turn for a sense of the aftermath of *EH*.

Heidegger was in a very different situation from Sartre. He himself insisted that he had been alienated from the Nazis for a long time. The authorities did not believe him – and he was banned until 1950 from teaching and was perhaps fortunate to escape worse consequences. From his compromise isolation, he replied to Sartre.

First Heidegger argues that all '-isms' are suspect, though useful for marketing purposes. That barb was clearly directed at Sartre – and at the accounts of his talk that had evidently reached Heidegger. From this bitter objection we can gauge the true impact of *EH*: Sartre had been the first to provide the post-war world with any kind of sense of a new '-ism'. In fact, as we have seen, this '-ism' – or these -isms – really expressed a deeply personal project. But by not making too directly personal a claim – offering say Sartreanism along the lines of Marxism or Freudianism – Sartre had made the ideas available to the wider world in an open form. He had set his own ideas free – in line with his own deepest principles.

So deep did Heidegger's objections run that he tried to coin a new language to escape from the one Sartre had rewoven:

> Such standing in the clearing of Being I call the ek-sistence of man.

In place of 'existence', Heidegger coins 'ek-sistence', a mix of ecstasy and existence. Once again, the effect is to pin down the specifically Sartrean flavour of the arguments in *EH*, the emphasis on struggle and strain and also the refusal to take on any religious consolation.

Heidegger then rewrote his central principle, about existence and essence:

> for ek-sistence is not the realization of an essence ... [but] the ecstatic relation to the clearing of Being.

In this context, he explicitly contrasts his own approach with that taken by Sartre in *EH*. Heidegger is trying to escape – as he sees it – from the nets of both existentialism and humanism. As we have seen throughout our reading of *EH*, Heidegger wants 'existence' to be a centre for a new mode of affirmation of our distinctively human way of belonging in the world – Dasein. Though no deity appears at the centre of this vision, there is a far more religious character to the approach than is compatible with Sartre's defiant atheism. Where Sartre proposed a philosophy of freedom, Heidegger tried to reconstruct a theory of belonging.

In that respect, he went on to insist that 'the thinking of *Being and Time is* against humanism' – if by humanism is meant anything like Sartre's conception of the individual seeking to make a new meaning from within the self. Heidegger talks rather of 'Man' as a whole and of his relation to 'Being' as a totality. The response gives a clear sense of what Sartre's *EH* represents – and does not represent – in modern thought.

Heidegger turns away from the Sartrean self – and looks instead to language. It is, he argues, in language that we come upon our relation to Being. Language is our distinctively human 'clearing' – the space from which we look round at the forest of being, seeing the different pathways that wind through it. In reaction to Sartre, Heidegger returns to a language of 'destiny' – in language we discover our human destiny, our illumination, our Being-in-the-World.

SARTRE'S FUTURES

After *EH*

* 1947 Publishes *Situations* I to be followed by ten further collections.

* 1947 *What Is Literature?* Series of theoretical essays comes out in his journal *Modern Times*, from February to July. Statement of his philosophy of committed literature, engagement.

* 1949   Adds *Iron in the Soul* to *The Roads to Freedom* instead of his earlier announced sequel.

* 1952   Sartre finally abandons the project of *Roads to Freedom*, leaving off the planned fourth book, *The Last Chance*.

* 1952   Publishes *Saint Genet.*

* 1960   *Critique of Dialectical Reason* (I) appears in May. Increasing association with politics of anti-colonial resistance. Writes Preface for *The Wretched of the Earth* by Frantz Fanon.

* 1964   Publishes the autobiographical *Words.*

* 1964   22 October Offered Nobel Prize for Literature. Rejects this prize and provokes outrage in France. Condemned as Soviet propagandist.

* 1971   May Publishes Part I of the massive life of Flaubert, *The Family Idiot.*

* 1973   Health failing. December Sartre loses sight.

* 1980   20 March Sartre collapses and taken into hospital. Dies 15 April. 19 April 50,000 people follow Sartre's coffin.

Sartre never again recovered quite that moment of influence – the solitary figure on the platform, the thinker amidst the ruins. Perhaps the rest of his career is overshadowed by that moment – struggling to re-create what was the outcome of a whole complex of forces, historical as well as personal.

REFERENCES AND FURTHER READING

The following works by Sartre have been cited:

Being and Nothingness, trans. by Hazel E. Barnes (Routledge, 1958).
Nausea, trans. by Robert Baldick (Penguin, 1965).
The Age of Reason, trans. by Eric Sutton (Penguin, 1986).
The Reprieve, trans. by Eric Sutton (Penguin, 1986).
Words, trans. by Irene Clephane (Penguin, 1967).
War Diaries, trans. by Quintin Hoare (Verso, 1999).
Modern Times: Selected Non-Fiction, trans. by Robin Buss, edited by
  Geoffrey Wall (Penguin, 2000).

The main biographical source has been:
Annie Cohen-Solal, *Sartre* (Gallimard, 1985).

Another lively biography:
Ronald Hayman, *Writing Against: A Biography of Sartre* (Weidenfeld
  & Nicolson, 1986).

A detailed account of Sartre and the post-war French setting:
Michael Scriven, *Jean-Paul Sartre: Politics and Culture in Postwar
  France* (Macmillan, 1999).

Good introductions to Sartre's thought:
Iris Murdoch, *Sartre: Romantic Rationalist* (Penguin, 1989).
Arthur Danto, *Sartre* (Fontana, 1985).
Christina Howells (ed.), *The Cambridge Companion to Sartre*
(Cambridge University Press, 1992).

More advanced accounts of Sartre's philosophy:
Joseph S. Catalano, *A Commentary on Jean-Paul Sartre's 'Being and
  Nothingness'* (University of Chicago Press, 1980).
Andrew Dobson, *Jean-Paul Sartre and the Politics of Reason* (Oxford
  University Press, 1993).
Mark Poster, *Existential Marxism in Post-War France: From Sartre to
  Althusser* (Princeton University Press, 1973).

For other philosophers, the following editions have been used and are recommended:

Martin Heidegger, *Being and Time*, trans. by John Macquarrie and Edward Robinson (Basil Blackwell, 1962).

Martin Heidegger, *Basic Writings*, ed. by David Farrell Krell (Routledge, 1993) – 'Letter' trans. by Frank Cappuzzi.

Immanuel Kant, *Grounding for the Metaphysic of Morals*, trans. by James W. Ellington (Hackett, 1981).

Soren Kierkegaard, *Fear and Trembling*, trans. by Walter Lowrie (Everyman, 1994).

Friedrich Nietzsche, *Thus Spake Zarathustra*, trans. by A. Tille and M. M. Bozman (Everyman, 1932).

Plato, *The Last Days of Socrates*, trans. by Hugh Tredennick and Harold Tarrant (Penguin, 1993).

INDEX